ALL THINGS ARE POSSIBLE
TODO ES POSIBLE

⊕

PLATINUM SPONSORS

From all the saints at MCC Washington, DC, past
(including Kerry Brown, the Buchanan brothers, Bob Johnson,
Ford Singletary, Sibbie Deal, Ida Salmon and Rev. Larry J. Uhrig),
present and especially future!

Universal Fellowship of Metropolitan Community Churches

GOLD SPONSORS

Rev. Jim Merritt and Al Leach

SILVER SPONSORS

All God's Children MCC, Minneapolis, MN
Church of the Trinity MCC, Sarasota, FL
Michael Dively

TROY PERRY
PASTOR AND PROPHET

⊕

Chris Glaser, Editor

Cathy Mijou, Designer

Metropolitan Community Churches

West Hollywood, California

© 2005 Metropolitan Community Churches

Scripture quotations, unless otherwise noted, are from the New Revised Standard Version of the Bible, copyright © 1989 by the Division of Christian Education of the National Council of the Churches of Christ in the U.S.A., and are used by permission. Spanish scripture quotations are from Nueva Versión Internacional, © 1984 by the International Bible Society, and are used by permission.

Troy Perry quotations are from *The Lord is My Shepherd and He Knows I'm Gay* © 1972 Troy D. Perry (25th Anniversary Edition, 1997, Universal Fellowship Press, Los Angeles, CA), *Don't Be Afraid Anymore* © 1990 Reverend Troy D. Perry (with Thomas L. P. Swicegood; Stonewall Inn Editions, St. Martin's Press, New York), and *Ten Spiritual Truths for Successful Living for Gays and Lesbians [...and everyone else!]: Discovering Positive Spirituality for Gays and Lesbians on the Journey of Faith* © 2003 by Troy D. Perry (Second Edition, Morris Publishing) and are used by permission. Quotes of Troy Perry, Alan Cranston, Barbara Gittings, and Henry Waxman are from *Speaking for Our Lives: Historic Speeches and Rhetoric for Gay and Lesbian Rights [1892-2000]*, Robert B. Ridinger, Editor © 2004 by The Haworth Press, Inc., Bingingham, New York, and are used by permission.

Edited by Chris Glaser
Book and cover design by Cathy Mijou
Introduction by Nancy Wilson
Preface and Afterword by Chris Glaser
Spanish Translation by Edgard Danielsen-Morales, Ph.D.

First Edition Published by Metropolitan Community Churches

Printed in the United States of America

Library of Congress Cataloging-in-Publication Data

Glaser, Chris, editor.
      Troy Perry: Pastor and Prophet/UFMCC - 1st ed.
      ISBN 0-9741793-1-0
      1. Homosexuality-Religious aspects-Christianity. I. Title.

In honor of the Reverend Troy D. Perry,

Founder of the

Universal Fellowship of Metropolitan Community Churches,

his supportive soul mate, Phillip Ray DeBlieck,

his loving mother, Edith Allen Perry,

and the members and congregations of UFMCC

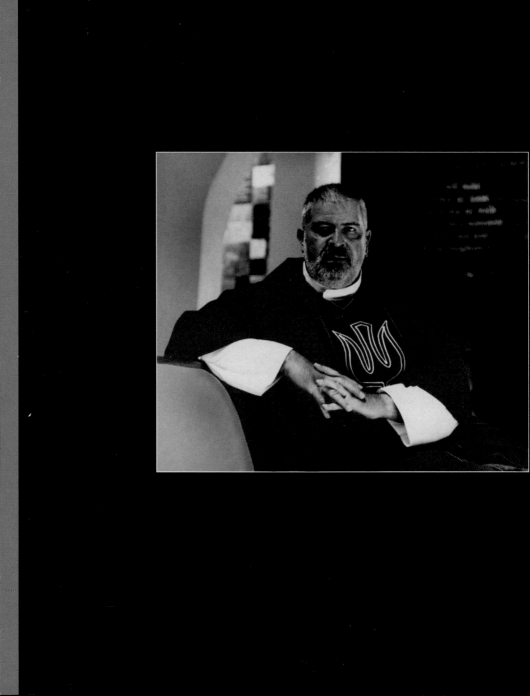

TROY PERRY
PASTOR AND PROPHET

PREFACE

My first encounter of the Reverend Troy Perry was similar to many of those whose lives he has touched: I received Holy Communion from him at an altar rail after hearing him proclaim that I as a gay person was welcome at Christ's table. It was in Sunday worship at the "Mother Church" during the 1972 Third General Conference of the Universal Fellowship of Metropolitan Community Churches (UFMCC), held in Los Angeles. Subsequently, I met him in an informal social setting, and mentioned my encounter to a gay friend. "My God, what did you say to him?" my very impressed friend wanted to know. "I didn't have to say anything to him," I replied, "He just sort of filled up the room!" Such is the charisma of the single most influential leader of the gay movement.

A professor of mine dramatically began his first lecture in an introductory course on the New Testament by declaring that what set early Christians apart from other nascent religious sects of the time was neither the superiority of their theology nor of their ethics. Rather, he declared, it was their experience of the power of the Holy Spirit. Indeed, as I later learned from another Bible teacher, in the story of Pentecost, the inspiration of the Holy Spirit not only empowers the disciples to proclaim the Gospel in the languages of strangers visiting Jerusalem, but also, in the story, it seems to make the walls of the room in which they huddle disappear, for they are suddenly outside on the streets where the strangers can hear them.

It was this pentecostal power that Troy Perry brought to bear in making closet walls disappear even as he built up Christ's Church. He did not found a separatist church, but a church that welcomed those whose love and sexual and gender identities were and are rejected by other religious institutions. He gave us the power of "that old time religion" in a new movement that would come to include gay men, lesbians, bisexual and transgender people, as well as our families, friends, and allies—a movement that would cross denominational, racial, gender, class, and national boundaries, as well as differences of age, appearance, and abilities. And he interpreted that old time religion into a new age of activism and public witness.

As a result, the UFMCC is the largest international gay organization. Conceived nine months before the birth of the Stonewall Rebellion, its counter-cultural companion, this denomination has influence well beyond its numbers. Long before I met the man behind it all, two of his parishioners came and spoke to my home Presbyterian church about their faith and their lives, impressing a standing-room-only crowd. From numerous expressions of this witness to the application for membership in the National Council of Churches, Troy Perry and UFMCC have served together prophetically on behalf of all of us in every denomination and tradition.

The suspicion and hostility of the gay community to things religious are understandable, given religion's history of spiritual abuse. But it has also prevented the gay community's full embrace and recognition of the Reverend Perry's accomplishments, not simply in founding a denomination, but in confronting religious justifications for bigotry, discrimination, and violence. Even many in the Fellowship do not fully comprehend that a giant walks among them.

And, in Troy's presence, it's easy for his friends to forget this, too. His humble and charming "down home" ways easily camouflage Christ's lion within, whose only absolute intolerance is toward intolerance itself. He is by no means Jesus, a lamb led to the slaughter, but he *is* reminiscent of a Paul, whose audacious confrontations and fierce pastoral tenderness toward the congregations he founded is writ large in scripture.

Generations of gay Christians to come will give thanks that God gave us a man like Troy Perry at this momentous time in gay history. In pictures, graphics, and text, this small book gives us a taste of his challenges and contributions until a definitive biography is produced. As an editor, I decided the most powerful way of experiencing this prophet and pastor was by selecting stories from his own accounts and those around him. As a writer, I respect Troy's gift not only in telling the Gospel story, but our own story—the story of a spiritual movement in church and society.

Unabashedly, I consider Troy Perry a saint—not in the sense some consider sainthood, a perfect person; but rather, in the sense that he risked his life and his livelihood to follow God's calling, and inspired others to do so. I thank God for Troy Perry, for his friendship and his inspiration, which has been expressed in a multitude of ways over the years, but most importantly, by his steadfast love for each of us, which is indeed a living reminder of the Christ he follows and proclaims.

Chris Glaser
Atlanta, Georgia

ACKNOWLEDGEMENTS

Designer Cathy Mijou proposed the original idea and subsequently designed the book. Nancy Wilson led the way in making the vision reality, seeking support and funding as well as overseeing the project. Because of his writing and publishing experience, she invited Chris Glaser to serve as editor, collecting text and photos, assisting with promotion. Connie Meadows generously gave of her administrative skills to coordinate the effort. Steve Jordan and Mark Hahn volunteered to gather photos for review. Jim Birkitt, Jim Mitulski, and Frank Zerilli assisted with information. K.C. McAlister assisted with research and provided support. Kerry Lobel and Cindi Love oversaw budget and coordination within the UFMCC staff. Generous donors covered many production costs. And, from his books, Troy Perry contributed the stories that drive the narrative, sometimes assisted in their telling by author Thomas Swicegood.

Thank you all for your time, talents, and contributions to the value of this project!

INTRODUCTION

———————⊕———————

In 1968, before Stonewall, homosexuality was a crime, a diagnosable mental illness and a sin so grave that few but the most fanatical ever spoke of it publicly. Homosexuals were to be pitied, punished, controlled and kept at the margins of "decent" community. It was a crime, in some states, for homosexuals to assemble publicly, and in some places, they were required to "register" with the police department as sex offenders. There were secretive organizations and a literal handful of people who were beginning to petition for civil rights, but who were not on the radar screen of the general public.

In the history of the gay rights movement (now the LGBT, or Queer movement) there is one person whose courage and consistent leadership stands out over nearly 40 years—and that is Troy Perry, the Founder of MCC. There is a saying, "History is the lengthened shadow of a great person." This man has cast an enormous shadow. Our book is one attempt to fathom that shadow.

In 1968, Troy Perry had the audacity to place an ad in *The Advocate* inviting

Hear
Rev.
Troy
D.
Perry

Every
Sunday
1:30pm

Metropolitan Community Church
Temporarily meeting at:
6205 Miles Ave., Huntington Park,
Phone: 581-9284   90255

homosexuals and anyone else who dared to come to a worship service in his home in Huntington Park, California.

Troy says he did this because he needed a safe, welcoming place to worship, and people with whom to worship. He says he had no idea that he would start a church movement that would sweep across 22 countries; that would inspire many imitators as well as an interfaith explosion of LGBT religious movements; that would rock the church, the nation, and the world, causing in 2004 the U.S. Congress to consider a Federal Amendment to the Constitution forbidding gay marriage and becoming an issue in elections in this country and many others.

Maybe it was a good thing he couldn't see all that far ahead of him.

In Troy's first book, *The Lord is My Shepherd and He Knows I'm Gay*, he stated in an open letter to the Church Universal: "I am not a monster. I am a human being, a man of flesh and blood." It is hard now to imagine anyone saying that in an age of *Ellen*, *Will and Grace*, *Queer Eye for the Straight Guy*, other gay characters on television, and debates about whether we should have full marriage equality or only the rights offered through civil unions.

Our vision in this book was to look back so that we might look forward. We want to understand from where we have come through the life work of Troy Perry. We wanted to show him in that amazing, angry, and determined stance photographed in the midst of the ruins of MCC Los Angeles after it had been burned to the ground by arsonists. We wanted to show him full of joy in that photo with Father Malcolm Boyd on the cover of *The Advocate* so many years after that first advertisement for MCC that used his high school photograph! We want to show his passion about MCC church plants in countries like Brazil.

Troy Perry is a person of great passion and zeal. Although he belongs to history, the history of the church and the world, and the Gay Rights Movement—first and foremost, we in MCC feel like he is ours. Through this book, we want to honor his legacy to us, and to celebrate the person who has led us for nearly four decades.

Primarily we know Troy Perry as a deeply spiritual person,

who exudes the unconditional love of God. Whether he is meeting with an Episcopal bishop, a Goddess worshiper, a local newspaper reporter, a prisoner, a U.S. president, or AIDS activists, he is always himself, and always, first and foremost, a person of deep faith and conviction. Troy Perry believes that MCC, the church movement that started in his home, is, in every way, completely, the Church of Jesus Christ: a Christ who is so much more inclusive than the church historically ever imagined, who identifies with those on the margins, and who, through us, works tirelessly for justice.

From that first worship service, Troy's genius of keeping the message of MCC strong, simple, and inclusive has worked. Someone urged him in those early days not to simply form a church out of his Pentecostal background, but to form a grassroots, ecumenical expression of church—which we have done in MCC.

In MCC's eclectic worship, you will see elements of the mass, Episcopal communion, contemporary Christian praise-and-worship, Methodist and Baptist hymns, liberation and feminist theology. From the beginning we were very amenable to interfaith dialogue and hospitality. MCC is the first church in the world that we know to sponsor the formation of a synagogue: Beth Chayim

Chadashim in Los Angeles, formed by Jews who had been attending MCC Los Angeles. Troy Perry helped find them their first rabbi. BCC, as it is still called, met at MCC Los Angeles in its early years. It was the first gay and lesbian Reform congregation in the world, and there are now over one hundred worldwide.

In the early days, many of the founders and leaders of denominational LGBT caucuses met each other, worshiped, and healed from the wounds of homophobia in MCC, while choosing to stay and work within their own communions. This is true of Chris Glaser, spiritual teacher and activist, our editor, always at home in MCC while continuing to challenge the Presbyterians from within. Bishop Carl Bean, Founder of Unity Fellowship, a self-consciously African-American LGBT congregation in Los Angeles that has become a national movement as well, traces his spiritual roots to MCC's early days.

Troy preached, in those first years, the three-part gospel that still functions as the core of the mission and values statement of MCC worldwide: The gospel of salvation, the gospel of community, and the gospel of Christian social action. It was gospel, "good news" that we could offer to a hurting and hungry community —a community that had heard nothing but "bad news" from the church. And from the beginning God has used Troy Perry's personality to drive this movement. His boundless energy and relentless optimism have sustained us through some incredibly difficult and challenging times. His vision of an international and self-consciously ecumenical and multi-cultural church movement is an entirely 21st century idea, born in the 20th century. While it is very anachronistic, in some ways, to be starting a new denomination, a post-denominational denomination like MCC has all the earmarks of a fresh new embodiment of "church."

Troy Perry always embodied the words of his first sermon, "Be True to You." He fills a room when he enters it. His charisma and capacity to say the right thing in the right moment have blessed so many. Many leaders in the LGBT civil rights movement (a surprising number of whom themselves come from religious backgrounds), turned to Troy as friend and pastor over the years. Leaders who struggled with AIDS or burnout or failure or grief or pain often turned to him, even if they were never officially members of MCC. They have relied on his consistency, his kindness, his energy and sometimes, on his faith.

And he loves the fight for justice, for human and civil rights for the LGBT

community and beyond. Troy has linked our struggles to the struggles for the rights of women, of prisoners, of the poor. He has spoken out consistently against the death penalty, and its racist and classist implementation in the United States.

Troy Perry has not been afraid to be challenged. He has modeled being a continuous learner, and we have learned with him.

Troy has never been ashamed or let fear control him or prevent him from taking on a challenge. He has never backed away from a struggle or backed down. He has told the truth as he perceived it, and has taken on some very tough battles, politically and spiritually. He taught us about spiritually-based activism and how it is inextricably tied to faith.

In the initial two years of MCC, Troy was arrested in one of the first demonstrations for gay civil rights in Los Angeles. In those days, even though MCC was in the news, many of those attending MCC and serving on the board were still in the closet. They were also not very familiar with the tactics of nonviolent resistance that included being arrested for civil disobedience, or very sophisticated about political activism. Troy was in his late twenties, with a board that included people old enough to be his father (they were all men at that time). His arrest frightened the board, and they fired him. When the

congregation heard this, they called a meeting, and promptly fired the board! Troy then asked the congregation to re-elect the board, because he believed in forgiveness, and that everyone had a learning curve, including those board members. His graciousness and maturity in that moment set a tone for leadership that has worked well for us. Some of those board members became part of the first Board of Elders of MCC worldwide.

Troy Perry was the first to see the marriage struggle as our struggle and to believe in it. When others put the issue on the back burner, or shied away from it, he took it on, early on. What is happening today around the world would not have happened were it not for his sacrifice, example, and influence. We have trusted his instincts about our movement and are glad we have. He performed the first public Holy Union, and MCC ministers perform 6,000 same-sex weddings annually. We would have no "marriage equality" movement were it not for that pioneering spirit.

Troy has also trusted us with his heart, his soul, his family. Troy shared his mother, Edith Allen Perry (1916-1989), with us. Before there was PFLAG, she was there, supportive, involved in civil rights, mothering so many who were orphaned by the homophobia of their biological parents. She was there in the first parades and in the front row at worship. In traveling with Troy to Australia and England she became one of the first heterosexual advocates and ambassadors, a mother who loved her son and "all my gay children."

And, Troy Perry has done all this without selling out or seeking personal gain. He has never been phony or pretentious. He is genuinely humble while modeling healthy self-esteem. He has never betrayed our trust, as have so many other religious leaders. When he makes a mistake, he owns it. He has shown us that asking for or offering forgiveness is a sign of strength in a leader, not weakness.

Troy Perry taught us to relax, even in church, and that it is okay to laugh and cry—in worship or in business meetings. Personal authenticity is critical to our movement and to healthy, sustained leadership.

Troy Perry encouraged us to learn to love and value freedom and be willing to take responsibility for our freedom. In the early days from the pulpit of MCC Los Angeles, and on the streets, he pushed and even bullied the congregation and the community to exercise their human and civil rights—to vote, to protest peaceably, to march, and to challenge wary politicians to view us as a constituency they had to reckon with. He went on television and radio and endless talk shows, one of the first to say publicly "I am a homosexual, I am a human being. You have nothing to fear from me." Later he would say of the gay community, of the MCC community "To know us is to love us."

Troy has always been proud of his southern, Baptist and Pentecostal roots. My own theory is that Troy is a true son of the early Pentecostal movement, whose origins were a working class/poor spiritual/religious/social movement in this country that crossed racial and eventually class boundaries. Only later was the Pentecostal movement taken over by fundamentalists and, in some cases, by those with strong racial prejudices. But it was the understanding of the Holy Spirit, its passion and freedom, that always undergirded Troy's personal spiritual life, and made possible the movement of the Spirit that we call MCC.

It was that amazing experience of being swept up by and in the Holy Spirit that so attracted me in those early days. As a northern (U.S.) Methodist, from the "frozen chosen" wing of the Protestant church in America, I was totally dazzled by the charismatic passion and power, combined with gay activism and an openness to feminist and liberation theology that was alive in MCC. To this day, for me there is nothing that compares with the grand opening worship service of an MCC General Conference, unless it is the evening healing service later during the same conference.

I met Troy the first weekend of February in 1973. I was 22 years old and in my first year of seminary at Boston School of Theology. I was on the front page of the Boston Globe in November of 1972 as one of the founders of the new MCC in Boston. The only reason I wasn't thrown out of Boston University that very week was because I had joined MCC and was not attempting to pursue Methodist credentials—and because a very brave professor and field education

director took me under his wing and protected me from the school's hierarchy.

Troy came to see us in Boston to give us our charter, and to officially bless me as a student minister. I met him at Arlington Street Unitarian Church, where MCC convened in the chapel. I remember how he filled the room, and felt amused that he looked a little like Elvis Presley, sideburns and all, in church drag. He jumped from his chair and hugged me. He has a way of greeting you that can make you feel like you are the most important person in the world.

Then, I heard him preach: that fascinating combination of Pentecostal fire and radical social justice and inclusivity sealed it for me that day. I knew I was "in the right place," that this was a movement in which I could grow. And if there was room for me, there was room for so many more.

Troy's visit came just one week after our church in Los Angeles had burned to the ground at the hands of arsonists, the first of 21 of our churches targeted by arsons and fire bombings over the years. It was a terrible time for MCC.

Troy was still the senior pastor of that church. He felt he had to go to Boston the next week, because he felt a calling to the world, to new communities, to a larger, urgent vision. He knew the MCC in Los Angeles would have to move on beyond his leadership, and that this new, fledgling worldwide movement needed him more. He left the L.A. church later that year and became full-time Moderator, a job that had no salary for the first two years.

We in MCC have leaned on and counted on Troy Perry to be there at the head of the parade, to be a friend and shepherd. Dear Troy, we have been selfish with you all these years— you have been "ours," but really, you belong to history, to the Church Universal, and to a world that continues to need your unique and passionate voice.

Troy Perry, we love you. Many of us believe we owe our lives and our ministries to you and your courage. All the tributes, photos, or words in the world cannot measure up to the immeasurable gift that you have been and will continue to be for as long as God gives you life!

The Reverend Elder Nancy Wilson
Church of the Trinity Metropolitan Community Church
Sarasota, Florida

UFMCC STATISTICS & INTERESTING FACTS

12 Worshipers at first service October 6, 1968

250 Self-governing congregations

10 Member international Board of Elders

43,000 Members as of 2004

23 Countries, 46 states have congregations; interest expressed in over 20 other countries

50.5% Clergy are women

20 Mainline seminaries train MCC clergy

$4 Million UFMCC World Center in West Hollywood, CA

6,000 Holy Unions annually

21 Congregations arsoned or fire-bombed

6,000 MCC members have died of AIDS

$20 million annual budget for all MCC congregations

$3.2 million annual budget for MCC headquarters and Regional Elders

2 Sacraments: Baptism and Holy Communion

6 Rites: Ordination, Membership, Holy Union/Matrimony, Funeral/Memorial Service, Laying on of Hands, Blessing

Reverend Troy Perry with the Board of Elders

MCC is the largest international vehicle for public education about homosexuality and Christianity.

Largest MCC is Joy MCC in Orlando, Florida, with more than 600 members.

Membership is inclusive of many heterosexual as well as LGBT members.

Membership is ecumenical, culturally and racially diverse, and includes people with disabilities.

Congregations welcome an increasing number of children of same-gender couples.

As early as 1970, MCC filed a lawsuit seeking legal recognition for same-gender couples.

The Board of Elders consists of a Moderator, Vice Moderator, and eight Regional Elders.

MCC has a congregational form of government, with local churches represented in an international General Conference which meets every two years.

MCC recently reorganized regions globally to ensure cultural diversity.

MCC and its Founder Troy Perry have been featured in major newspapers, magazines, television and radio programs in the United States and abroad.

REVEREND TROY PERRY CHRONOLOGY

1940	Born in Tallahassee, Florida
1953	Began preaching at 13
1955	Licensed as a Baptist minister at 15
1959	Married his pastor's daughter
1960	Moved to Illinois with wife and son to attend Midwest Bible College
1962	Moved by his employer to Southern California with wife and two sons
	Became pastor of the Church of God of Prophecy in Santa Ana
1964	Came out; separated from wife
1965	Drafted into U.S. army
1967	Honorably discharged
1968	Founded first MCC congregation at his home in Los Angeles October 6
1969	Performed the first public same-sex wedding ceremony in the United Sates
1970	First fast on the steps of the Federal Building in Los Angeles
	Filed the first lawsuit seeking legal recognition of same-sex marriages
1971	Consecrated first church owned by MCC at Twenty-second and Union in Los Angeles; first property owned by a GLBT organization in the U.S.
	Participated in first March on Sacramento, California's capital
1972	Became Moderator of the new Universal Fellowship of Metropolitan Community Churches
	Published *The Lord Is My Shepherd and He Knows I'm Gay*
	First international missionary trip: Great Britain
1973	MCC Los Angeles church burned by arson

Brought healing to New Orleans after The Upstairs bar was arsoned, killing 29   **1973**
Second international missionary trip: Australia   **1974**
Appointed to the Los Angeles Commission for Human Rights   **1976**
Invited to the White House by President Jimmy Carter to discuss civil rights   **1977**
Addressed religious issues raised by Anita Bryant opposing gay rights in Florida

Second fast at the Federal Building in Los Angeles
Leader in the "No on Proposition Six" campaign in California   **1978**
Received Humanitarian Award from the ACLU's Lesbian and
Gay Rights Chapter
Rode the "Freedom Train" to first March on Washington;   **1979**
addressed people at stops as well as the marchers
UFMCC applied for membership in the National Council of Churches   **1981**
Challenged religious demagogues declaring AIDS as God's
punishment as pandemic begins
Preached at the National Council of Churches   **1983**
Completed one-hour video, "God, Gays, & the Gospel: This Is Our Story"   **1984**
Met partner-in-life Phillip DeBlieck "who has since brightened my life"   **1985**
Contributed slogan to the second March on Washington: **1987**
"For love or life, we're not going back."
Celebrated Holy Communion at the Lincoln Memorial and
participated at the wedding of two thousand couples.
Invited to "quasi-ecumenical" mass celebrated by
Pope John Paul II in Columbia, South Carolina
Published *Don't Be Afraid Anymore: The Story of Reverend*   **1990**
Troy Perry and the Metropolitan Community Churches with
Thomas L.P. Swicegood

1990	UFMCC given observer status in the World Council of Churches
1993	Invited by President Bill Clinton to the first White House Conference on AIDS
1997	Named official delegate by President Bill Clinton to the White House Conference on Hate Crimes
	One of 100 U.S. spiritual leaders honored by President Clinton at White House breakfast.
2000	Led UFMCC and more than 200 LGBT organizations in creating the Millennium March on Washington; addressed 800,000 marchers
2003	Published *Ten Spiritual Truths for Successful Living for Gays and Lesbians (and every one else!): Discovering Positive Spirituality for Gays and Lesbians on the Journey of Faith*
	Received the Humanitarian Award of the Gay Press Association
	Received honorary degree from Episcopal Divinity School in Cambridge, Massachusetts
	Married longtime partner Phillip DeBlieck in Toronto, Canada
2004	With his partner of 20 years, Phillip DeBlieck, and with lesbian couple Robin Tyler and Diane Olson, filed the first modern day lawsuit in California seeking legal recognition of same-sex marriages
2005	A California judge rules in favor of his 2004 lawsuit, making same-sex marriage legal in California, thirty-six years after he performed the first public same-sex wedding
	Retiring as founding Moderator of the UFMCC

Reverend Troy Perry *by artist Steed Taylor*

Who will separate us from the love of Christ?

Will hardship, or distress, or persecution,

or famine, or nakedness, or peril, or sword?

I am convinced that neither death nor life,

nor angels, nor rulers,

nor things present, nor things to come,

nor powers,

nor height, nor depth,

nor anything else in all creation,

will be able to separate us from the love of God

in Christ Jesus our Lord.

- Romans 8:35, 38-39

Life is a journey.

We are all on our separate paths which weave and wind together.

We would be lost without luminaries on the way.

Troy has been one not only in what he said and did but simply by being who he is.

He gave hope, light, and life, and we thank God for him and all he has meant to those who have known and loved him.

God bless you.

+Desmond M. Tutu
Archbishop Emeritus of South Africa
Nobel Peace Laureate

CHAPTER ONE
THE CALL

———⊕———

"You knit me together in my mother's womb..."
- Psalm 139:13

Born July 27, 1940, Tallahassee, Florida.

"If the doctor had told me, when Troy was born, that he was a homosexual—that he'd grow up to be one—I couldn't have loved him any less than I did, nor than I do now..."   - Edith Allen Perry

My father was the type of man who was convinced that nothing was impossible. I substituted my talking to God for talks I had previously enjoyed with my father.

~✿~

Keeping us together as a family shows the kind of real strength my mother had. We were down and out, but we held together. My brothers and I learned a lot from it. Nothing would ever drive us apart after that. I think that's one of the reasons my brothers stood by me, without any question, when the whole thing about my being a gay minister came out.

~✧~

The way Jesus wore his hair was not so much hippie as feminine. As I studied the portrait, I overwhelmingly liked this Israelite. I felt that we had something in common. We were not well understood by men; we were outcasts.

~✧~

At age ten, I was attending prayer services on every occasion without prompting. I often won prizes for memorizing Scripture. There was something wonderful about worship, friendly Southern people, and congregational dinners. But then my stepfather came along and made me quit. He said church was a place for sissies.

Aunt Lizzy not only became a pillar of her church, she became the church. Everyone wanted to hear her speak. She inspired everyone. She had her own radio show. She didn't organize well. But she seemed to mesmerize them all. She was also the snake handler in the family.

"Just be you. Be yourself. Be what you want to be; and let others say, think, or do what they want," Aunt Lizzy always advised me. So she must have had a tremendous influence on my early religious searchings. It is an influence that stays with me now. She was the first to say that I would preach.

She announced that she had been given most certain knowledge that I was called to reveal and preach the Will of God. She placed her hands on the top of my head. "God has His hands on this boy," she told us all. "Henceforth," she added, "You, Troy Perry, shall also be of such an understanding." Why did I cry? I don't really know. I was afraid, but I felt a happy weight of oncoming responsibility.

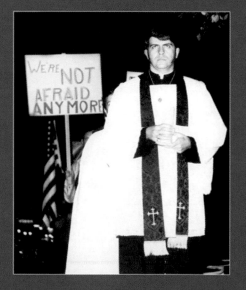

Now the word of the Lord came to me saying,
"Before I formed you in the womb I knew you, and
before you were born I consecrated you;
I appointed you a prophet to the nations."
Then I said, "Ah, Lord God! Truly I do not
know how to speak, for I am only a boy."
But the Lord said to me,
"Do not say, 'I am only a boy':
for you shall go to all to whom I send you,
and you shall speak whatever I command you,
Do not be afraid of them,
for I am with you to deliver you,
says the Lord."

- Jeremiah 1:4-8

That night I had to preach. Behind my uncle's house, there was a large cornfield. I walked out into it, thinking of what I would say. I went to the end of the cornfield, opened the Bible, and started to preach to the corn stalks. I preached of divine love. I told the corn stalks that God loved them. As I spoke, I saw a large blackbird light on one of the corn stalks. I was sure that this was

a demon from Hell. I picked up a long stick. I rebuked it in the name of Jesus. I struck once, and then again and again. The bird flew away. I had succeeded only in destroying the cornstalk.

When I was fifteen, I got my license to preach. Even in junior high, I had preached at least once a week. I held chapel services every Tuesday morning. I was enrolled at Murphy High School where I annoyed teachers as well as students by forever preaching Salvation on the entrance steps. I remember that summer in 1956, when I was just 16. I became a paid evangelist, traveling throughout Alabama, preaching. "Why, God, would you let me have those feelings even before I knew I was called to preach?" I knew that somewhere, somehow my strong physical attraction for the masculine image that I carried with me would find an answering reflection.

~☆~

In 1961, there was a witch hunt going on throughout Florida. It came about through the Johns Commission, appointed by the state legislature to investigate and root out homosexuality in Florida, and to expose it. Mr. Johns, who headed the commission, was later appointed governor. Johns and his people published a pamphlet called, "Homosexuality and Citizenship in Florida." It was an exposé. As a result of the report, the slightest breath of scandal about homosexuality could ruin a person, forever. People were called up in front of judges and asked about homosexual acts and homosexual people they knew. People with well-established jobs or from prominent families just disappeared.

~☆~

 I enrolled in night classes at the Moody Bible Institute.

~☆~

"Troy, you can never again be a minister for the Church of God," the regional overseer explained. "Don't you realize that the Church of God says that once you've been thrown out for homosexuality, you can never be in it again?'

I replied, "You forgive adultery—and that is breaking one of the Ten Commandments!"

"But," he said, "I'm sure that's something God understands."

~☆~

I settled in California. I was pastor of my own flock. I was already twenty-three.

Being a queer was the most horrible thing in American society.

~✧~

I finally went up to the woman behind the counter, and said to her, "Tell me something. Do you have any books on homosexuality?" I turned to *The Homosexual in America*, by Donald Webster Cory. When I finished the book, I knew without the shadow of a doubt that I was a homosexual; I was gay. And there was just nothing for me to be afraid of any longer. The first thing it meant was that I knew I had to resign the pastorate of my church.

~✧~

"I don't think it bothers the good Lord, so why should it bother you?" - Willie Smith.

For God so loved the world... - John 3:16a

Willie Smith was the first homosexual man with whom I became acquainted in Hollywood. "God loves me!" was Willie's steadfast belief. Therefore, with contagious conviction, he was able to say, "Listen, Troy, you are a homosexual. You will always be a homosexual until the day you die. God knows that you are a homosexual. God made you the way you are, and God loves you! Nothing you or I can do will change it!"

Another friend caused me to do something I had never considered before. I entered a bar. It was a gay establishment called The Islander, located in Huntington Park. When I drank my first beer, all of my Pentecostal fears came forward, and I was afraid God might strike me dead on the spot! Two years later, in 1965, I was drafted into the U.S. Army, which refused to believe my outspoken assertions of being homosexual.

~☆~

My God, my God, why have you forsaken me? - Psalm 22:1

~☆~

At L.A. County General Hospital, I was sitting, crying uncontrollably. This person reached down and stuck a magazine into my hands and said, "Here, some of us care!" I looked up dumbly, and stared at this black woman. "I don't know why you did this," the woman said as my eyes turned toward hers, but what you did tonight was crazy—why don't you look up?"

With my Pentecostal background, I knew the nurse's words meant, "Why don't you get your act together and get in touch with God?"

And she added, "You're too young for this sort of thing!" Then the woman showed me scars on her wrists. "I did it, too, one time. But I went on and I made something out of myself. You should do the same. Get hold of yourself. Nothing can be that bad!"

It was just like a slap in the face. It snapped me out of my depression, just to hear that someone cared. Then the lady left. I never knew her name, but, when I was aware that she had gone, I remembered God. It took my acceptance of my own homosexuality for me to realize that all the barriers of prejudice must come down.

When I was alone, I tried talking to our Creator again. One of my biggest stumbling blocks was that I had fallen out of love with God. Larry was my new object of worship and adoration. For the first time in my life I began to have a growing, uneasy sense of failure. I had lost something I had loved more than anything else in the world. That was the problem of course. Larry had taken God's place. I said, "You know, God, I'm awfully sorry. You know I learned to love and worship somebody more than I worshiped you. Now, I ask you to forgive me."

Instantly, the peace and joy that I had felt with God before returned. The effect was so sudden that I was close to becoming frightened. "Wait a minute, God!" I exclaimed. "I don't know what you expect from me—I'm still a homosexual—a practicing homosexual!"

Then God spoke to my heart, and God said to me,

"Troy, do not tell me what I can and cannot do.

I love you. You are my son.

I do not have stepdaughters or stepsons!"

CHAPTER TWO

THE GOSPEL

"I have other sheep that do not belong to this fold.
I must bring them also, and they will listen to my voice.
So there will be one flock, one shepherd."
- Jesus in John 10:16

"When Troy stood up to be counted with his
gay brothers and sisters, and when he found
his mission in this life, I figured that he was
doing what he knew in his own mind was right.
And I'm with him all the way."
- Edith Allen Perry

It was apparent from my first Los Angeles
Times story on the Metropolitan Community
Church in late 1969 that yet another historical religious movement was

emerging in Southern California. Who but Troy Perry would have had the wisdom and energy to give the UFMCC such a solid base?"
- John Dart, news editor, *Christian Century*, author of *Decoding Mark*

I asked for some sign from God. I remember in my prayers I would ask God where I fit into His plans, what the work was that he had set out for me. I worried about going to church. I couldn't get over the loneliness I felt, being out of it all. How could the church not pray for me? I felt that they had let me down.

~☼~

Then I heard the voice of the Lord saying, "Whom shall I send, and who will go for us?" And I said, "Here am I; send me!"
- Isaiah 6:8

~☼~

Tony growled, "You know, Troy, I've learned one thing from this experience, nobody likes a queer. We're just a bunch of dirty queers and nobody cares about dirty queers!

"Somebody cares."

"Who?"

"God cares."

Tony just laughed bitterly, and said, "Oh, come on, Troy, God doesn't care about me." With that, he turned and left. I knelt down and said, "All right, God, if it's Your will; if You want to see a church started as an outreach into our community, You just let me know when." And that still, small voice let me know—*now!*

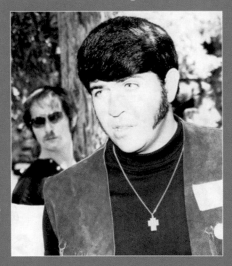

~✵~

One thing is sure. We homosexuals must all learn to rid ourselves of the sense of shame that we have been conditioned to accept from the heterosexual world. Such shame is no longer acceptable to any of us. How could we go on being ashamed of something that God created?

~✵~

I knew that the mission was coming into focus. God wanted me to start a new church that would reach into the gay community, but that would include anyone and everyone. I knew that the word "church" would be in the title. Then I would ask the Lord if it was to be really an outreach into the gay community. So the word "community" got into the title. Community meant a feeling of comradeship, a small area, a place where you knew everybody. So, it would be a community church. We would also serve a large community; we would serve the whole Los Angeles area, so the word "metropolitan" finally came to mind.

"How're you going to organize a bunch of queens? Nobody has ever organized the gay community into anything and accomplished anything." - Willie Smith

It was October 6, 1968. There were twelve in the living room, and I walked out and asked everyone to stand up, and I said, "We'll go before the Lord in prayer." We joined hands and prayed. Then I said, "We'll sing some hymns." No one knew what to expect. Everyone was as scared as I was. I introduced the church. I said the church was organized to serve the religious, spiritual, and social needs of the homosexual community of greater Los Angeles, but I expected it to grow to reach homosexuals wherever they might be. I made it clear that we were not a gay church—we were a Christian church, and I said that in my first sermon. I told our gathering what Metropolitan Community Church was going to be; and I told them I would preach what God had told me to preach, a three-pronged Gospel: Salvation, Community, Christian Social Action.

An Answer to a Mother's Prayer

"Seven years later, after a worship service at our church in Sydney, Australia, a lesbian in her sixties and her friend came to me with tears in their eyes. 'I've got to tell you a story,' the older woman said, and although I had never met either of them, I immediately felt as if we had known each other for a long time.

"'Until recently, I was head of women's ministry in the Anglican church,' the lesbian told me. 'They didn't ordain women, of course, but we had input where women's issues were concerned. On one occasion, I was called and asked to go to a home to be with a neighborhood woman who had just discovered that her only son, who was gay, had killed himself. The date was the sixth of October, 1968. I remember it very well. I was dreadfully shaken because I knew I was also gay, a secret which at that time I had never divulged to anyone. I remember getting down on

my knees beside the dead son's bed and consoling his mother. There was a note saying he was taking his life because he was homosexual and could no longer suffer being unacceptable.

"His mother said, 'I pray that someday, somehow, someone will bring into existence a church that will accept gay people and let them know they don't have to do this—that God loves them!" And now, seven years later, here you are in Sydney. God bless you.'

"Then I told the kind lesbian the remaining part of the story, which she didn't know, that the first worship service of Metropolitan Community Church had taken place in America on October 6, 1968—the exact date as the mother's prayer!"

- Reverend Lee Carlton

Although I became pastor and founder, I don't really feel like a pastor, at least not in the sense I'm used to thinking of pastoring. I am an exhorter, a preacher from the pulpit, an evangelist.

"I just want to stay with two main rules: Love God, and help your fellow human beings. Keep the doctrine down to a mild roar, and avoid a lot of rules."

- Willie Smith

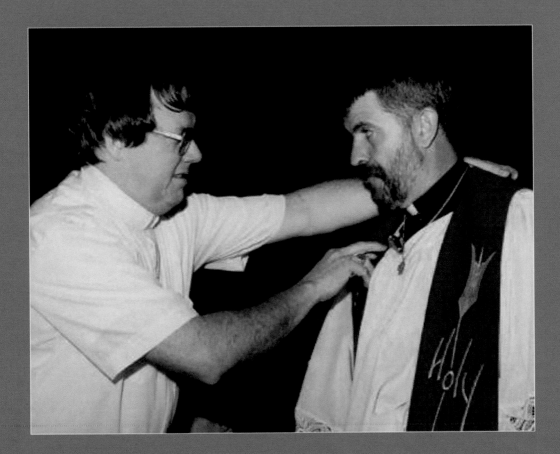

"I am a lapsed high church Episcopalian, whatever that means. And I came here to see what kind of fraud was being perpetrated. I had read about you and the church in The Advocate. *I really came to sneer. But I am stunned to see your congregation made up of Catholics, all Protestant sects, and Jews. Truly, MCC means 'catholic' and even more than that."*

- Bill Thorne

~☆~

About forty years ago a wind of liberation began to blow. This wind of liberation was of the Holy Spirit. The most profound and difficult aspect of that liberation was on the spiritual level. Gay people throughout the world had internalized the condemnation that came from various religious traditions. To carry out gay liberation the Holy Spirit had need of human instruments with a special kind of holiness. First of all, the Spirit had to find gays and lesbians who, because of their profound faith in God's love, had freed themselves from the self rejection of church teaching and had come through to self acceptance. Then the Spirit needed to find men and women with deep humility, a humility that would allow them to accomplish extraordinary things through the Spirit's power without letting it go to their heads. All the glory of their accomplishments had to return to God and not to their ego.

God found such a man in Troy Perry. I am convinced that Troy Perry was God's

*primary instrument in
bringing about gay liberation
for the past forty years. My
initial encounter with Troy
was nearly thirty years ago
when I was on a tour with my
first book,* The Church and
the Homosexual. *When I
arrived in Los Angeles, Troy
invited me to lunch, listened
carefully to what I had to say,
and offered me his support
for my work within the
Roman Catholic Church. We*

Charles Chiarelli, Troy Perry and John McNeill

*have had thirty years of a collaborative ministry since that time. With Troy's
support and encouragement I have found a welcome in Metropolitan
Community Churches all over this country and Canada. He made me feel
welcome at the national conference in Phoenix in July 1993. In my present
exile status within the Roman Catholic Church I have found a spiritual home in
the MCC in Fort Lauderdale: Sunshine Cathedral. Every day in my prayers I
thank God for Troy Perry and all that he has done to support my ministry and*

all he is doing to help liberate my gay brothers and lesbian sisters all over the world. He is a priceless treasure in our midst.

- John J. McNeill, Co-founder of Dignity, New York City, and author of four books, including his latest, an autobiography, *Both Feet Firmly Planted in Midair*

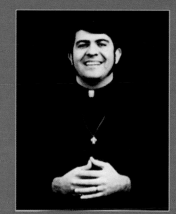

When he walked down the aisle dressed in the black robe, and the white cassock, and sang the hymn at the top of his voice, it bowled us over. That shock of black hair, the piercing, smiling eyes and the puckish grin charmed us all. We could feel the thrill of being cast under this man's personal spell; his personal experience with God reached all of us.
- An African-American entertainer

"Troy Perry's ministry with the Metropolitan Community Church of Los Angeles was already underway when, as a seminary senior, I came out publicly in 1970. We both remember those early days when even lesbian, gay, bisexual and transgender people viewed 'gay ministers' as aliens. But we had work to do. Troy's visionary leadership of the Universal Fellowship of Metropolitan

Community Churches and his immediate, strong voice against injustice are hallmarks of his ministry. For nearly four decades, he has resolutely spoken

our truths to church and state leaders who did not want to hear.

But it is Troy's pastoral heart, which has always acutely felt the pain of our people, that most impresses me. This is a good and loving man whose ministry has saved many lives, in the United States and throughout the world. His witness has blessed our communities in ways we will probably never fully know. It is difficult to calculate the debt of gratitude, of respect and of love that our whole community owes to Troy. As he retires, may the younger generation of religious and community leaders take inspiration from his example, not merely to emulate him, but to live their lives as authentically as he has lived his."

- Reverend William R. Johnson, Ed.D., first openly gay person ordained within a conference of the United Church of Christ in 1972.

We were gathering strength even from the people who ignored us or tossed us out of our church homes. Every time someone asked us to move, it only brought us new people.

~☆~

I am not a patient man. The building fund for our first church grew slowly, far too slowly. So one Sunday, I preached and challenged the congregation to raise $10,000 in one week's time. I wanted to see it there by next Sunday.

Sunday, October 19, 1969 filled me with tingling excitement. I had to know not *if* my prayers were answered, but *how*. So great was my faith in God and the congregation that I had brought a twenty-gallon trash can to collect the money. We would all march by it and give what we could. I asked if someone could play that old-time hymn, "Give Me That Old Time Religion."

The church treasurer and his helpers went upstairs and counted the money during the last part of the service. We waited. I had a lump in my throat. Someone handed me a piece of paper. I puzzled a moment over the message. I read, "The count isn't complete. The change hasn't been counted, but we are a little over the $10,000 mark already." I looked out over the congregation, a sea of faces lost in the lights that illuminated the altar. The light didn't blind me. Tears did. There was a long, awesome silence. Someone jumped up and yelled, "THANK YOU, JEEZUS!" Wave after wave of applause shook the Encore Theater to its foundations. The organist started playing, "Praise God From Whom All Blessings Flow."

~☆~

On that day, as I bowed my head, I saw that the sunlight streaming in through the great stained-glass windows and the interior lighting make the church glow with a golden hue. I go forward, changing the mood. Sometimes I think it's a little bit of a shame to break up such a pleasant and prayerful meditation. But I feel so full of energy, and I love these people so much. I respond to them, as they do to me. We give each other energy and the strength and courage to go on. I feel sure of myself, but I know that it comes from the inspiration that God gives me. It warms me so. And that warmth fills the room. It always does.

You are cordially invited to attend the Dedication of the Metropolitan Community Church, The Mother Church

2201 South Union Avenue, Los Angeles, California on Sunday, March 7, 1971, at 11.00 a.m.

Rev. Troy D. Perry Pastor and Founder

"If you love the Lord this morning, would you say, amen!"
"Amens" pour out and sprinkle my talks and my sermons like
salt. "If we get to the point where we forget God,
and we remember just ourselves,
and we put us on the pedestal, and we say,
'Look what we've done'
and forget it was God who did it for us, we'll fail!"

"Troy Perry has been a signal blessing at two critical stages of my life. First, when I was a deeply closeted, heterosexually married fundamentalist browsing in a Manhattan bookstore with my mother and a friend. I saw Troy's book, The Lord Is My Shepherd and He Knows I'm Gay. *My first thought: "This is blasphemy!" My second thought: "This is my story!" I asked my friend to distract my mother while I purchased the book. Reading it was my very first step toward accepting the person I was created to be.*

"Much later, still closeted but co-author of Is the Homosexual My Neighbor? *and actively advocating for gay liberation, I spoke at a UFMCC conference where I was pressured to come out more publicly. I had been trying to build a scholarly reputation academically and theologically, and did not yet feel the time was right for coming out. Knowing about those pressures, when Troy hugged me, he whispered, 'Right now we need you <u>exactly where you are</u>.' With his timely encouragement, I waited until all internal systems said 'go' before telling everyone who would listen exactly who I am by the grace of God.*

"Thank you, Troy. You are indeed <u>reverend</u>."

- Virginia Ramey Mollenkott, Ph.D., transgender lesbian activist, lecturer, author of 13 books and hundreds of articles.

"Mr. Speaker, on June 26, the Metropolitan Community Church of Los Angeles will mark 'Gay Pride Sunday' with a special service of celebration and the conferring of special honors on the denomination's founder, Rev. Troy D. Perry.

"The denomination founded by Troy Perry, the Universal Fellowship of Metropolitan Community Churches, is one of the most unusual religious organizations in the world. It is dedicated to extending to members of the gay community the spiritual guidance and religious fellowship so often unavailable to them in the mainstream 'straight' churches.

"Rev. Perry, himself a gay, had to build his church in the face of tremendous hostility from other clergy and deep doubts within the gay community as to whether such an unusual institution could succeed.

"Few people have done more than Rev. Troy Perry to give to gays a sense of self-worth and an ability to fulfill joyfully and without guilt or social rejection their most profound religious needs."

- Representative Henry Waxman,
Congressional Record, June 9, 1977

Immediately upon my arrival in Los Angeles, I departed for the desert, a vast expanse of sand, wasteland, cactus, and distant purple mountains. I was alone, miles from the town of Twentynine Palms, in a deserted campground with only coyotes and jackrabbits keeping me company. There were no great visions, but within my being I reaffirmed my knowledge that I had to keep our Fellowship firmly rooted in doctrine. Some of our pastors had sought to become more unitarian and less evangelical, but our Lord let me realize in the majesty of God's living desert that so long as our church continued to follow Jesus, all would be well.

My denomination was also in a major struggle concerning the use of inclusive language. "Is God both mother and father to us?" was one of the questions that has been of serious concern to many religions. The answer was not easy, particularly because of centuries of male-dominated tradition. But as I fasted and prayed, I came to understand that God is not a woman, not a man. God is both, but neither. When Moses asked God, "Who shall I say sent me?" God replied, "Tell them 'I am' sent you. I am that I am."

Some women in our community, particularly feminists, felt that the generic words *gay* and *homosexual* did not apply to them, and wanted to be called lesbians instead. Other women felt strongly that use of the word *gay* should not be handed over to the male segment of our population. Personally, I have no problem with either usage. Outside of Twentynine Palms, however, with the sun and the night and wind and rain to sharpen my perception, God let me know that words which anybody considered exclusionary or offensive should not be used in preaching the Gospel. Thus, I came to the decision that, from then on, whatever language will reach the largest number of people is the language Metropolitan Community Church will use.

Thus, I came to the decision that,

from then on, whatever language will reach

the largest number of people is the language

Metropolitan Community Church will use.

CHAPTER THREE

THE MINISTRY

---⊕---

"We knew that the worship of God comes from the heart."
- The Reverend Troy Perry

"It surely took a lot of thinking and praying to realize that many of the old strict ways in which we were raised just aren't what it's all about. The real sins are hate and being inhuman to each other. That's how we all sin against homosexuals."
- Edith Allen Perry

In the second year of our congregation's existence, when the Universal Fellowship of Metropolitan Community Churches came into being and I became its moderator, my mother had come to live with me, and we survived on the small salary I received. Sometimes we were hungry. For a while we existed on a limited diet of spaghetti and canned asparagus which charitable members had donated to what was called the Deacon's Closet. Our congregation was, for the most part, blissfully unaware that their pastor and his family were forced to feed themselves with provisions for the needy.

~✧~

The church, which had grown with vitality from its infancy, suddenly was threatened with becoming nonevangelical: conservative members struggled for a retreat toward social invisibility. After we bought, renovated, and consecrated our first church, the imposing edifice which stood at the corner of Twenty-second and Union in Los Angeles, many of us thought we had accomplished our final objective. Somewhere along the way many of us, myself included, had developed the habit of saying that MCC's only reason for being was to encourage long-established denominations to reexamine their homophobic interpretations of theology. Many of us who should have known better more than once commented, "We are working to work ourselves out of business."

After nearly four years of existence, when our Third General Conference was held in Los Angeles during the Labor Day weekend, we

were at a crossroads. The year was 1972, and it happened that an analytical business-management consultant, an ex-Mormon on the threshold of becoming one of our ordained ministers, quietly challenged the overall perception of what Metropolitan Community Church should become. On September 3, the final day of our gathering, Jim Sandmire, was scheduled to preach the main sermon. Fifteen-hundred people were present.

"If Metropolitan Community Church is here to stay," he preached, *"I urge an end to middle-class introversion and the beginning of a greater commitment to opening the Fellowship to more young people, to more heterosexuals, more minority groups, and a lot more women!"*

Applause ensued. Jim smiled in his own thoughtful, unhurried manner, and then continued, "We should not be concerned that different churches in our

Fellowship may adopt varying spiritual trappings. Devotion need not be a wholly rigid ritual."

A milestone had also been reached during that meeting: the Reverend Freda Smith became the first woman in our denomination to be officially licensed as a minister.

"In those days, before Metropolitan Community Church, before the Stonewall Rebellion, before June days were dedicated to gay pride, it was so easy to hate oneself. It was so typical to say, 'I should have been more careful—I lost my job because somewhere I let my guard down and was noticed—I lost my job because I associated with people who were too obvious—it was all my fault!' But actually, it was the system's fault, although we rarely thought or said that in the 1960s! ... It was my conclusion that any people who were oppressed, particularly gay people like myself, could not depend upon others to be our heroes."

- Reverend Freda Smith

"LGBTQ Christians would still be sitting in the pews of oppressive churches listening to homophobic sermons if the Reverend Troy Perry had not listened to the Spirit of Love. Instead, we are living out our faith in inclusive, welcoming and justice-focused communities. Troy invited us to be church, and church we are!"

- Mary E. Hunt, feminist theologian and co-director of the Women's Alliance for Theology, Ethics and Ritual (WATER)

"I met Reverend Perry some 30 years ago at a UFMCC General Conference in Denver, Colorado. The moment he said hello to me I felt at home. Over the years I have trusted him with my life. That trust has proved to be well-founded. There are many stories that I would love to tell. But, this story moves me the most—how Reverend Perry treated his mother and my mother.

"My mother, Mrs. Inez Berry was Mama Berry to all who knew her. She was a dear friend to Reverend Perry's mother, known by all as Mother Perry. His love for his mother was so moving, it blessed all who saw it. She raised her son to give his heart to mothers and fathers who loved their LGTB children. I am speaking of a time when many families threw us away. Our mothers were dear friends. Both of these soft, strong women were from the same cloth. They loved their children with a passion that goes beyond words. My mother loved her Troy. He always took time to let Mama know that he carried her in his heart. She just claimed him as her own. She loved to pray for him and his mother. He gave my mother a respect that caused her heart to sing. I still have gifts he gave her. When she crossed over, Reverend Perry preached at Mama's celebration of life. She had always said, 'I feel like he's one of my children. He loves me and I am blessed.'"

- Reverend Delores Berry, Full-time Evangelist for UFMCC since 1987

Judy Kiser, Delores Berry, Troy Perry and Phillip DeBlieck

"Reverend Troy Perry has been a wonderful friend and teacher. When I came back to Los Angeles as its first openly lesbian rabbi in 1988, Troy invited me to speak at the annual MCC dinner in October and give the invocation, strengthening the bonds between the Jewish gay community and UFMCC. (It was Troy who helped found the first gay temple in Los Angeles.) I'll never forget that invitation, nor his words to me that expressed his own pride at finally having an openly lesbian person as a rabbi.

"Through the years we've marched together, prayed together, protested together, delivered invocations for President Clinton together, laughed together, raised money together, and most of all shared a strong friendship together. May God continue to bless him with health and long life and to smile upon him and his family with shalom-peace."

- Rabbi Denise L. Eger, founding rabbi of Congregation Kol Ami in West Hollywood, California

"Reverend Perry?"

"Yes?" I answered nervously.

"Twenty-second and Union is involved in a major-alarm fire. Seventeen units have responded."

The words were like a knife plunged into my stomach.

The Reverend Lee Carlton, pastor of the L.A. church, was waiting when we deplaned. He saw me hurrying off the ramp and shouted my name. I thought he wanted to say more after that, but for the moment his speech failed. Instead, he threw his arms around me and began to sob. Words became unnecessary. Our church at the corner of Twenty-second and Union had been an important building. It was the first property ever owned by any gay organization in America—but it was much more than a building! We had performed services of Holy Union there. We had buried our dead from there. We had made it a wellspring for rejoicing and communion. It had been our center—and it was destroyed...

It was all gone! I kicked my foot in the ashes. I thought, Dear God, when will people ever leave us alone? Why should anyone feel compelled to commit such a desecration? Why can't people, no matter what their belief, listen to the message of Jesus? Why do too many people find *love* so impossible to understand?

While those and similar bleak thoughts raced through my mind, I realized I was crying. I looked up at Willie Smith. Willie's face was filled with compassion, but there was strength, too. "My God, Troy!" Willie exclaimed, trying not to lose patience with me,

"The Church didn't burn down!

These ruins are just the closet.

Look at all of us out here in the open—

we are the Church!"

Seventeen sites where we have worshiped have been intentionally burned, three in 1973 alone. The third fire was by far the worst, a nightmare in a city where unsuspected intolerance festered like an unclean wound. It occurred the last Sunday of June 1973, Gay Pride Day in many U.S. cities.

The Reverend John Gill, southeastern district coordinator for the Fellowship, reached me by phone late that evening. "There's been a terrible fire," he said, "They were having a beer bust late in the afternoon—you know, all you can eat and drink for a dollar, with lots of people in the bar, crowded, typical of New Orleans. It's a place called the UpStairs, same location where MCC used to hold prayer meetings. Some of our members were there."

"Tell me nobody's hurt!" I exclaimed.

Reverend Gill sighed. "You realize I don't have many details here in Georgia. I'll know more after I arrive in New Orleans, from all first reports, it's serious."

"What does that mean?"

"It means people are dead."

"How many?"

"I don't know. More than twenty. Maybe fifty. Many are burned beyond recognition."

I began to feel sick.

"What I know, Troy, boils down to just this: a lot of gay people are dead, and more than a dozen badly burned survivors have been taken to the hospital." Reverend Gill lost his composure and began crying into the telephone. "Can you meet me in New Orleans?" he asked.

"On the first available flight," I replied, rubbing my head which had begun to ache.

"Seven o'clock was the official end of the beer bust. When it was over, there was a tradition in the bar for everyone to link their arms together and sing:

United we stand, divided we fall—
And if our backs should ever be against the wall,
We will be together—
Together—you and I.

The lucky ones went home. About sixty, or more, remained."

- André, a survivor

"What tragedy? I don't know any tragedy. Only some faggots got burned!"

\- A man at the airport

"I hope the fire burned their dresses off."

\- A bigot

*"The Lord had something to do with this.
He caught them and punished them."*

\- A "Christian" woman

"They were my sisters and brothers who were destroyed in the fire. They are at peace now. They are joined with Jesus. It is the individual or individuals who committed this crime— they are the ones we have to pray for."

\- The Reverend Troy Perry

"I want to tell you something!" I said angrily to the reporters. "I've seen yellow journalism before, and quotes from cops in your newspapers and on television about the UpStairs being a queer bar and a hangout for thieves won't do. The words are un—ack—ept—able!"

Gay entrepreneurs suddenly wanted to have a meeting with those of us who had come into their city. "How dare you hold your damn news conferences!" one of them demanded. Looking at him and his mercenary associates, who had never done anything to repay the gay community for wealth they derived from it, I felt a growing warmth under my collar. "The reason I'm here is because when it comes to city officials and business leaders like you, I find you're a greedy lot that cares about nobody but yourselves." They, however, were not my primary disappointment. That dubious honor went to churches...

~☆~

"Here's [my lover] Kay [Lahusen]'s book, The Gay Crusaders, *published in 1972. Troy Perry's is the first interview, and it opens quoting him, "When people call me the gay Billy Graham, I say—No, he's the straight Troy Perry."*

A few years later, when Troy and I were both serving on the board of directors of the National Gay Task Force, several of us went to a meeting with top executives at NBC to complain about the lack of gay programming.

You know how such meetings go. We're polite, they're polite. We explain, they explain. We ask, they demur. We push, they postpone.

Then Troy spoke up. He said—and I'm sorry. I can't do the accent: "I've just come back from a trip to Australia, and one of their TV soap operas has a gay male couple who is having problems in their relationship. And do you know, every afternoon 13 million Australians are on the edge of their chairs to see if Jack and Tom can work it out!"

You should have seen their eyes. Troy hit the NBC people right where it mattered—hooking an audience. In two sentences Troy got through to them after all our rational negotiation rolled off their backs. I think most gay movement people outside MCC have been slow to appreciate the power of Troy's direct appeal.

Now I come to my own moment of embarrassment with Troy Perry. I don't remember the date. The Philadelphia MCC was in trouble: it had been through three pastors in two years. Troy came here to mend the trouble. I recall that his viewpoint, his solution, wasn't acceptable to the members of the congregation. But I don't remember what the exact issue was. Anyway, I found myself siding with my friends in the church here.

There was a meeting with Troy Perry at the Joseph Priestly Chapel here at First Unitarian. I attended to give support to my friends in the congregation. The atmosphere was very tense. In the middle of one heated exchange, I piped up and called Troy a Neanderthal. You could have heard the hairpins drop.

The sequel is even more embarrassing. After Reverend Joseph Gilbert came to this MCC church, he once asked me, "What's this I hear about your calling Troy Perry a Neanderthal?" I denied it. "Oh, I never said that," I claimed.

Later Joe came at me another way. "Say, Barbara, about that time you called Troy a Neanderthal. Was the meeting in this room or that one?" "Oh, it was that one."

Back to the moment in the chapel. Troy is a real Christian. He forgave me, at *least I think he forgave me. What's more he converted me. I have had only good to say about him since.*

What I think of Troy today is what I've known all these twenty years (except for that one mad moment): Troy is a national gay treasure who is underappreciated. And we're going to need him more than ever if Anita Bryant's comeback picks up any steam."

- Barbara Gittings, founder of the Lesbian/Gay Roundtable of the American Library Association, June 15, 1990. Quoted in *Speaking for Our Lives: Historic Speeches and Rhetoric for Gay and Lesbian Rights (1892-2000)*

"But we have this treasure in earthen vessels, so that it may be made clear that this extraordinary power belongs to God and does not come from us. We are afflicted in every way, but not crushed; perplexed, but not driven to despair; persecuted, but not forsaken; struck down, but not destroyed; always carrying in the body the death of Jesus, so that the life of Jesus may also be made visible in our bodies."

- 2 Corinthians 4:7-10

Reverend Jeri Ann Harvey received concerned telephone calls from several excited members of her Houston congregation. "The television stations and the radio stations are broadcasting the Ku Klux Klan's phone number," one of our members said. "They're asking people to dial a recorded message. It's bad. They're giving the KKK free publicity."

"So what's the message?" Jeri Ann asked.

"The KKK's calling for the death of every homosexual in Texas!"

"They want to kill 'pansy preachers'!" The message mentioned the Houston MCC specifically, giving the address.

The next morning, Jeri Ann had planned to go to the church at her usual time of nine o'clock, but the church secretary had arrived early, and phoned her at seven-thirty.

"They've burned a cross on our front lawn," she exclaimed.

The cross was made of iron pipes and rusty rebar wrapped in heavy burlap. The burlap had been enclosed with chicken wire. Inside this bulky assembly were .22- and .38-caliber bullets. It had been doused with kerosene and set on fire during the darkest hours of night.

Several threatening phone calls ensued, both at the church and Reverend Harvey's unlisted home phone. "I sat up all night in the kitchen with a thirty-eight," she described the evening that followed. "My lover was awake in the living room with a twenty-two. At any moment we expected our doors to be broken down. Several days passed that way, until hysterical, I called Troy. In those days, when we had trouble in our little churches, we could call Los Angeles and 'Daddy' would usually come running to help."

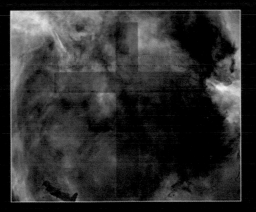

The Washington Post story one wintry, snowy day in December of 1970 reported that I, besides proclaiming that God loves gay people, would be in the nation's capital to perform a holy union, often referred to as a "gay marriage" in the press. The Episcopal bishop was a reader of The Post and, on his forceful orders, we were, without any notice or prior warning, locked out in the snow, unable to enter the church the Reverend Paul Breton had rented for the afternoon. I told the newsman, "We are going to pray for the soul of the Episcopal bishop who denied shelter to this small band of Christians you see here, locked out in the freezing cold. The bishop is in need of salvation, and in order to pray for him, we are now on our way to the National Cathedral!"

Reverend Breton's head swiveled in my direction. "We are?" he said.

"Yes," I replied with bravado to accompany my sudden inspiration.

Our congregation had dwindled to eight when we arrived at the cathedral, but the press corps and television crews with their cameras had somehow increased. We worked our way through the crowds into the sanctuary. As I entered a wide aisle which led directly to the iron fence, a youthful clergyman appeared from off to the side and blocked my progress. Before I could say anything to him, his eyes widened appreciably, and I could see a glint of friendly recognition. Unexpectedly, a warm smile appeared on his face and, in a loud whisper, he asked, "You're Reverend Troy Perry, aren't you? I am so happy to meet you! I'm an Episcopal seminary student and I've read all about you in *The Advocate*. Why are you here?"

I explained, and a sly, conspirational glint brightened his features. "Would you like to pass inside that iron gate and use our main altar?" The Episcopal seminary student who opened the gate to the altar for us was Jack Isbell, who later was ordained as one of our ministers, and served the Washington church with distinction.

Once inside, I fell on my knees and thanked God for watching over us. I began to pray. Quiet spread through the inner recesses of the National Cathedral. Tourists who had been moving aimlessly, took seats in the pews, and some knelt. Eventually I stood and, with both arms raised, faced the assembled crowd: "God, I want you to cure the Episcopal bishop of his homophobia. Throughout the world we suffer under the yoke of civil and religious oppression! So, Lord, we ask now that you release us. Set homosexuals free! Amen!"

Amid gasps of shock, tourists hastened for the nearest exits. Neither Jack Isbell nor I ever again emptied people from a building so fast in all our lives!

~☆~

Reverend Steve Pieters was director of our denomination's AIDS ministry. The doctors had said Steve would not live beyond 1984. He had been diagnosed with lymphoma and Kaposi's sarcoma. And then something miraculous happened to Steve.

Ten years later, in 1994, Steve was invited with 13 other leaders of AIDS/HIV religious organizations, to the White House by President Bill Clinton. Steve was invited to a breakfast meeting with the President and Vice President Al Gore. Steve was placed at the table next to Mr. Clinton and across from the Vice President. The President talked to Steve throughout breakfast. Steve told the President his story of his fight with AIDS/HIV and how he had almost died eleven years before. The President asked, "Steve, what do you attribute to the fact that you have had two kinds of cancer go into remission and are one of the longest survivors of AIDS in America?"

"Well," Steve began, "My doctors believe that the experimental drug Suramin, which everyone else in my control group died from, somehow helped me."

"But what do you believe?" the President asked.

"I believe that God touched my body and gave me healing," Steve answered.

We who are part of MCC believe in healing that comes to us by way of doctors and drugs. We also believe in healing that takes place even when the doctors have given up. We believe that God is greater than any disease.

"Yea, though I walk through the valley of the
shadow of death, I will fear no evil: for thou
art with me; thy rod and thy staff
they comfort me."

- Psalm 23:4 (KJV)

Gary Wilson was a member of the Mother Church. He was a young bodybuilder and sang in our choir. When he moved from Los Angeles, he transferred his membership, always remaining close to our churches. Then, unfortunately, in San Francisco, he contracted AIDS. Afterward, we had a conversation I will never forget.

Toward the end of his life, he told me, "I want to remind you that you preached a sermon years ago, that as Christians we have a choice of going first class or with no class at all! Do you recall?" I did. "Reverend Perry, I want to tell you I'm going first class! Even in death, I'm going first class! I know all that God has done for me in the past."

When the end was imminent, I called to pray with him over the telephone. He was very ill. "I don't think I'm going to make it much longer, Reverend Perry, but I want to tell you, I am going to do the best I can. I know that death is close, but I'm going first class. I told you that all along."

Then Gary, with his sweet spirit that never faltered in faith, said something I was not expecting. He said, "Reverend Perry, I'm going to make the transition. Do you have any messages? Is there some person on the other side you want me to say hello to?"

For 15 or 20 seconds I was unable to speak. When my voice returned, I said, "Gary, you know a lot of folks I love are on the other side. Please tell them I said hello, and tell them we're on our way there, too. Someday all of us will meet in that heavenly city, the New Jerusalem, just inside the eastern gate."

Two weeks later, one of the last things Gary Wilson said to friends who were gathered with him was, "Tell Reverend Perry that I went first class." Then he passed on into eternal life.

"See, the home of God is among mortals.

God will dwell with them as their God;

they will be God's peoples,

and God's own self will be with them;

God will wipe every tear from their eyes.

Death will be no more;

mourning and crying and pain will be no more,

for the first things have passed away."

\- Revelation 21:3-4

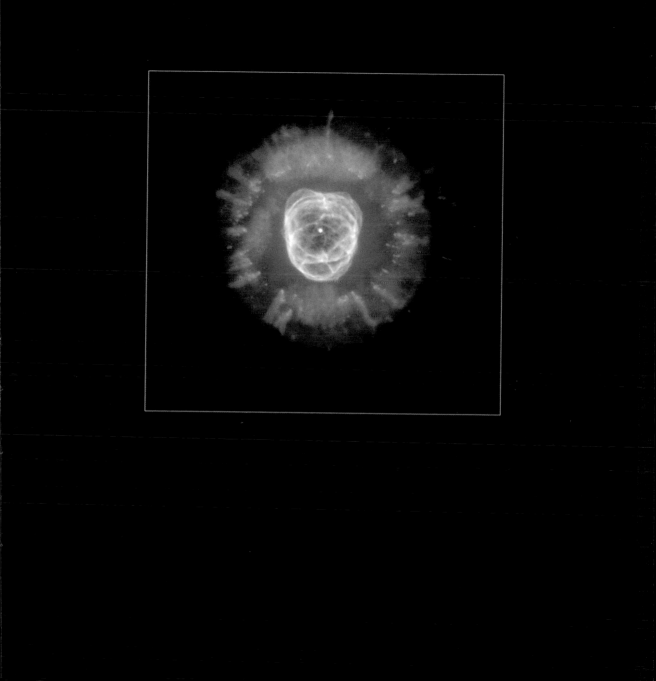

CHAPTER FOUR
THE MISSION:
ACTIVISM, ECUMENISM, EVANGELISM

⊕

What does the Lord require of you
but to do justice, and to love kindness
and to walk humbly with your God?
- Micah 6:8

"I have finally found my mission in this life."
- The Reverend Troy Perry

"I've met the nicest people I've ever met in my life as a result of Troy's work."
- Edith Allen Perry

I am not a creature from the outer darkness, as you seem to believe. I am a
homosexual, and like the members of your churches, a man of flesh and blood.
I am a member of the church, and an integral part of its people. If you will not
let me worship God in your temples, I will worship God in the cathedral of my

heart, and build for Him a temple where others can worship with me. I call upon all churches to assume their responsibility to broaden horizons, challenge the status quo, and when necessary, to alter social morality to enable God in Christ to work more effectively.

~☆~

You must know first that you are a human being, and you must learn that you have your rights, too, and they don't mean anything unless you're willing to fight for them.

~☆~

In April of 1969 we were visited by plainclothes vice squad officers. They had come by to look us over. A certain man was running for public office in Los Angeles, and part of his campaign was to attack the gay community. The police had come at his behest. They tried to loiter in the restrooms, if you can imagine that, during a church service. Now I never tell anyone how to vote, but I did say that since that certain man was running, if anyone voted for him, they'd almost surely die and go to hell. We campaigned actively against him. And he lost.

~☆~

I remember our first real social. We didn't really know how it would work out. Should we have dancing, which was illegal between people of the same sex in Los Angeles?

~☆~

Our first great test of courage came, I think, when we were nine months old. It was in April, 1969. We were asked to stand up and be counted and to stand for homosexual civil rights, to demonstrate in front of the Los Angeles offices

of State Steamship Lines. In San Francisco they had fired a young man because he was a homosexual. We numbered only eight, and we didn't know what would happen. We gathered with placards that we had made. So we marched. I was dressed in my most conservative dark suit, with a clerical collar. During the lunch break, when people came out of the building by the hundreds, we got some really cold stares. One person near me said, "Oh my God, the fairies have flown down from Hollywood." They jeered at us. We heard words like "queers," "faggots," "fairies," "sissies"; words I'd forgotten and some words that I'm not going to use in print. We smiled back. Once in a while I would say, "God bless you." Bags of water started dropping down from the roof of the building. Have you ever been hit with a bag of water? It can knock you out. The second day was just like the first. Day number three was something else. By this time, some of the people were making friends with us.

Not all members of my church felt as I did, that we had to take a militant, nonviolent stand against the kind of dehumanizing brutality and harassment we were up against. But those of us who had been through it knew that we would never be pushed again without standing up for our rights. We would never stand in the shadows. We would never hide our faces again. We would stand in the sunshine. We would know that God was with us, and that we were His children.

On Flag Day, June 14, 1970, I stunned my congregation, irritated some of my board of directors, and set off on a

crusade. I was determined to embark upon a fast until we had a really meaningful dialogue about changing the unjust laws that were used to harass and discriminate against homosexuals.

When it starts getting rough, that's when I work the best. And I tell you that my God is bigger than the Los Angeles Police Department. He's bigger than the state of California. He's bigger than the United States Government. We called the American Civil Liberties Union, and they entered the case. We're going to hold that parade! June the 28th!

June the 28th, after the parade, I'm starting a fast. And I'm sitting down on a corner on Hollywood Boulevard ...

~☆~

I took up my post on the steps of the Federal Building in downtown Los Angeles. I had a jug of water, an air mattress, a blanket, my Bible, and a Book of Common Prayer. ... I wanted someone in the power structure to come and talk about what was wrong, and what could be done about it. ... After ten days of my prayer-vigil and fast, I didn't know how long I could really hold out, but my fast ended that day. Three city councilmen came and visited me. They wanted a list of grievances on police harassment, police brutality,  unfair law enforcement, and discriminatory practices on the local level. They also promised to push for law reform through the legislature. They wanted to enter into a continuing dialogue with us. It was a personal victory. But more important, it was a victory of the whole gay community. I felt that it was fulfilling God's mission.

"I first met Troy on the steps of the California State Capitol in 1971. It was the day Assemblyman Willie Brown first introduced the Consenting Adults Bill, which would ultimately decriminalize gay and lesbian love in the state of

California. There was a rainbow around the sun that day. Assemblyman Brown said, 'I've heard about gay power, but this is amazing.'

"Troy was amazing, too, to the openly lesbian feminist but closeted charismatic evangelical Christian speaker—me—who stood beside him as we addressed the crowd. Never forget—Troy was barely 30 years old on that day. The founder and moderator of a movement he had visioned into being at the age of 28, calling it by the unbelievable name Universal Fellowship of Metropolitan Community Churches, boldly reaching across legal, denominational, color, and gender lines—Troy opened the door for me to reach out to women in ministry throughout the world, not as a token but rather, a foot in the door."

- Reverend Elder Freda Smith, Pastor of MCC Sacramento's Cathedral of Promise, was the first woman ordained to the MCC ministry. She served five terms on the Board of Elders beginning in 1973.

A very real fear engulfed gay Americans in 1977. On Cadillacs in Miami, bumper stickers appeared with white letters on a field of black, reading KILL A QUEER FOR CHRIST. Reigning over Miami's frenzy of self-righteousness and bigotry was Anita Bryant Green. Her antigay campaign began when she first lobbied against Dade County's Metro Commission, which intended to pass an ordinance forbidding discrimination against homosexuals in housing, public accommodation, and employment. Nonetheless the ordinance passed. A decision to seek a county referendum for repeal was immediately proposed. The choice for a public figure to front the campaign was Anita Bryant, then spokesperson for the Florida orange industry.

Gay leaders refused to consider that the "gays are going to hell" language Anita Bryant was using could really do our cause any harm. My opinion was the opposite. If Anita could use a few selected scriptures to condemn us, someone should quote better scriptures in our defense! Dade County voters went to the polls in record numbers on June 7, 1977, and almost 70

percent of them cast ballots against us! Gay people, in public and in private, were shocked. Thousands upon thousands of our sisters and brothers in Los Angeles, New York, San Francisco, Chicago, Dallas, Washington, D.C., and elsewhere took to the streets and held candlelight vigils. The steamroller of fear and falsehood kept advancing: Wichita, Kansas; St. Paul, Minnesota; Eugene, Oregon; California state senator John Briggs ... If the issue was freedom and justice for *all*, not just gay rights for us, we had a chance to win.

~☆~

On a flight, a very efficient airline stewardess asked if I would like orange juice for breakfast, and I inquired, "What kind of orange juice is it?"

"Sir?" she looked puzzled, "What do you mean?"

"I mean, is it from California? Or are the oranges from Arizona or Texas? Or from Florida? What state does it come from?"

"Does it really matter, sir?"

I smiled my broadest smile. "Yes, it matters. Will you find out for me?" I said in a stage whisper, aware that my fellow passengers were listening.

NO MORE ORANGE JUICE FROM THE UN-SHINE STATE

The stewardess returned. "The carton says it's Minute Maid but it doesn't have any state name on it," she said.

"I know what Minute Maid is. It's a blend containing Florida orange juice—and there's no way I can drink it!"

"Why can't you drink it?" she asked.

"Because I'm a homosexual," I replied. "Gay men and lesbians are boycotting the Florida citrus industry because of what Anita Bryant's been doing in that state."

The stewardess took it away. Not many minutes later, the stewardess returned. She had a friendly young steward in tow.

"Reverend Perry," he said with a twinkle in his eyes, "We'd be pleased if you'd come forward and take another seat. We think you'll be more comfortable in the cabin for first class passengers.

Naturally, I agreed.

~✧~

"You're not going to believe this," Reverend Eastman said, "The Hyatt called about your dinner reservations."

"Is there a problem?"

"Anita Bryant is going to be in the restaurant at the same time we are. The staff intends to seat us right next to the Bryant group, so you can speak to her if you wish."

In the restaurant, people seated with me kept asking, "What are you going to do, Troy?"

"Troy," said one of my dinner guests, "God doesn't speak to me in an audible

voice as he does you. Even so, I believe God must have put you and that woman together in this restaurant for a reason."

We noticed that people at other tables were not being served. Restaurant personnel, with a few brief exceptions, were watching me.

They had decided something was going to happen. I felt it would be a shame to disappoint everyone.

"Let's surprise her," I said to Reverend Eastman. Anita turned, looking over her shoulder. We had never met. "Miss Bryant," I said, "I'm Reverend Troy Perry of Metropolitan Community Church."

The smile froze on Anita's face, but the difference was barely perceptible. She was a typical Southerner, polite to a fault. "Oh, yes, you are the gentleman who debated Brother Bill in Miami," she said,"Let me introduce you to everyone here." Don and I shook hands around the group.

"Please, don't let me further delay your dinner," I said. "I just wanted to say that tragic things are happening to many people. In the interest of everybody, I think it's time for you and me to sit together and discuss the myths that surround this issue."

She said, "I'm sure than can be arranged."

But it never happened.

In 1975, I was one of about eighty persons, activists of every sort, who were invited to meet with Jimmy Carter in Los Angeles. Although few seemed to be taking Georgia's ex-governor seriously at the time, Carter was nevertheless seeking the Democratic Party's nomination to run for President of the United States. During lunch, Governor Carter stood at the head table and stated, "I will answer any questions you have." Since the majority of people present were activists of some sort, their topics covered the standard subjects. Then I stood and asked *the* question.

"Governor Carter," I said, "I have something my community would like to know.

 If you become president of the United States, are you willing to sign an executive order to ban discrimination against homosexuals in the areas of the military, housing, employment, and immigration?"

Instantly the noise level in the room dropped so that small sounds, like the clink of a glass, became magnified. Waiters stopped moving around. I heard a loud whisper off to the side asking, "Who let him in?" Taut faces everywhere turned and stared in my direction.

Of all the people in the room, the only one who registered no shock whatsoever was Jimmy Carter. With an amused glint in his eyes, he smiled, and in his deliberate fashion said, "Yes, I can answer your question, but you talk kind of fast—although I can tell you're a Southerner. Where are you from?"

"Florida," I replied.

"I thought so," said Carter. "I could be supportive of all those areas except one. The place I would have difficulty with is the area of employment where security clearances are involved, when there are employees who are not open about being gay."

Many months later, when Jimmy Carter was elected thirty-ninth president of the United States, I received a personal invitation to his inauguration. And, of course, I was very pleased to attend.

In 1977, there was another invitation to the District of Columbia, less ceremonial, but also with the blessing of President Carter. The event was a meeting consisting of individuals representing various gay interests throughout the United States, with a fact-finding mission to determine and begin the resolution of problems concerning homosexuals in America. The idea

was conceived by co-executive directors of the National Gay Task Force, Bruce Voeller and a brilliant ex-nun lesbian, Jean O'Leary. They worked in harmony with Midge Costanza, the first woman appointed Assistant to the President in American history, with whom we met.

Afterward, while leaving, I had to wipe tears from my eyes as I told my colleagues, "Just never forget how momentous is what has happened today! How few people in the world, even in America, ever really get to meet with their government? It's the validation of every American's dream!"

A follow-up meeting was held in Washington with the president's religious liaison, a Southern Baptist preacher. He expected only members of MCC. However, I asked Reverend Nancy Wilson and Mr. Adam DeBaugh to organize

the participants, and as a result of their planning, the White House was surprised by a list we presented of people coming to Washington: gay Mormons, gay Lutherans, gay Seventh Day Adventists, gay Catholics, gay Jews, gay Jehovah's Witnesses, gay Methodists, gay Presbyterians, and gays of the Greek Orthodox church. When the meeting was finished, the Southern Baptist religious liaison declared, "You have broken every stereotype I've ever had about homosexuals!"

When I was appointed by County Supervisor Ed Edelman to serve as a member

of the Los Angeles Commission for Human Rights, no openly gay person in America had ever been appointed to any type of commission. In protest, half of the existing members of the commission refused to come to my swearing in. Yet after three years, when I had successfully completed my work, the result was that many new doors were open for lesbian and gay people who wanted to serve thereafter.

In 1978, I received from the American Civil Liberties Union an award for commitment and leadership in the field of civil rights. The award was made by Alan Cranston, California's U.S. Senator. Twelve hundred people were present at the Hollywood Palladium. "Isn't it interesting," said Senator Cranston, "What crazy laws concerning homosexuals are still on the books in some of our states? Do you know that in Kansas, in this so-called enlightened day and age, it is still against the law for Troy Perry to drive a taxicab?"

"The tribute that you pay to Troy Perry has been earned through hard and selfless work to improve the lives of others, the lives of oppressed human beings. Having earned this tribute, one would think that Troy Perry would be standing in what Hubert Humphrey called 'the bright sunshine of human rights' which is the very promise of our democratic society—that Troy Perry's own human rights had not been violated. Far from it.

"This man that you are honoring, whose work has benefited so many, is a second-class citizen of a society that he nonetheless respects and serves. ... Most public and all private employers can refuse Troy Perry a job. Landlords can deny him an apartment or a house. All branches of the armed forces can refuse him the right to serve his country, and refuse him the right to visit members of his church who are inmates. Troy Perry can be barred from teaching, from practicing law, from being a doctor of medicine, or even from driving a cab. He can have his application for credit denied. He can be refused insurance. For Troy Perry—and for millions of others who share with him one characteristic—the bright sunshine of human rights is trapped behind the clouds of ignorance, intolerance, bigotry and fear."

- Senator Alan Cranston, in *Speaking for Our Lives: Historic Speeches and Rhetoric for Gay and Lesbian Rights*

In 1978, gay activists began suggesting a great march into Washington, D.C. In no way demeaning is the little-known fact that the idea for the march began with what was intended to be a joke. Robin Tyler was performing in Minneapolis. Some humorous lines she intended to use were: "I think we should march on Washington. We'll set up tents. We know how gay men love camping."

However, what the audience of four hundred lesbians and gay men heard was somewhat abbreviated.

"I think we should march on Washington," were the only words Robin had spoken when the people in the crowd, which believed they had heard a genuine call for action, spontaneously jumped to their feet and started cheering wildly. In tune with the unexpected excitement, Robin alertly cut her punch line and went along with a growing chant: "March on Washington! March on Washington!"

Our demands of the leaders of the United States would be (1) a national Gay and Lesbian Civil Rights Bill, (2) repeal of existing antigay laws, (3) an executive order from the president banning military, federal, and federally-related discrimination on the basis of sexual orientation, (4) an end to unfair bias in gay father and lesbian mother custody cases, and (5) the protection of lesbian and male homosexuals youths from discriminatory legislation.

October 14, 1979 was set as the date for our march. From San Francisco, an Amtrak train, dubbed "the Freedom train," offered gay camaraderie and an affordable ticket across the North American continent to Washington, D.C. I intended to travel using more expedient air transportation —until a self-described "radical, feminist, Jewish dyke" invited me to dinner and changed my mind. "Troy, there's going to be a special train to Washington," Robin Tyler began. "Why don't you and I go on board, and every time the train stops, we'll do a whistle-stop thing, à la Franklin and Eleanor Roosevelt? We'll go out on the caboose at the back of the train and give a little speech in every big town or hick city where the train stops, day or night, across country."

There was no rear platform on the Amtrak train from which to address the crowd; nevertheless, even if the schedule only allowed three or four minutes, we would hop off and give our speeches. The result was always tears and laughter. And sometimes people were so filled with joy from seeing a train packed with gay people that they impulsively decided to join us. They jumped aboard, and bought themselves a ticket to the first of the great gay marches in Washington, D.C.!"

Some members of the march committee were opposed to having a "gay clergyman" speak. Yet, as my friends will tell you, I was not prepared to leave quietly or remain silent. Nor was I content to be the thirty-seventh speaker who would probably be addressing remnants of a crowd long since departed!

"Don't worry, Troy," Robin said to me. "You will not be speaker number thirty-seven. You will be first! I'm the emcee, and I'll do what I think is right, once I get up on the stand." And do what she wanted, Robin Tyler did.

"We have had our setbacks," I told the crowd. "We lost to Anita Bryant in Dade County, Florida, and we're still smarting from civil rights losses in

Wichita, Kansas, St. Paul, Minnesota, and Eugene, Oregon. But we turned it around in California. That's important to remember. There have been setbacks, and there will be more setbacks, but in the end, we will win because we are right!"

"I first met Troy on the 'Gay Train' from San Francisco to the first national March on Washington, October 14, 1979—one

hundred and forty gay men and lesbians took over most of an Amtrak train across the country. We were met by cheering MCC members on stops along the way, but after a wonderful rally with sleepy MCCers at 4:00 a.m. in Ogden, Utah, a fundamentalist Christian anti-gay minister jumped onto the track in protest to block our departure. He chanted ugly slogans and carried a big ol' sign that said GOD HATES GAYS. GO HOME.

"The contrast was stark between his hatefulness and the love and cheers of the small but hearty LGBT crowd that had greeted us. The engineer and train staff—whom by then we had completely won over, especially with our nightly show-tune sing-alongs at the piano in the club car—didn't know what to do.

"But Troy did. He walked out on the platform and engaged the other minister— man of God to man of God—quietly and strongly. I don't know what he said, but within a few minutes, the other minister shrugged and then hefted himself (Troy was in far better shape than that other guy!) up on the platform and slipped away. Loud hurrahs and cheers erupted from the train and the platform and soon we were on our way.

"In the quarter century since that time, I have seen Troy speak often, read his words, and watched with admiration his significant work through MCC steadily

grow as the issue of gay rights has spread to the faith community, and as more and more LGBT folks have owned and evolved our own spirituality. His life-saving, visionary work and legacy can never be captured in words. He is one major reason that the LGBT movement for equality has had such awesome power and impact during the most conservative era in American history.

"We needed God on our side to defeat them, and I believe Troy was sent to us for that reason. He has been a leader for all of us. And, in addition, his legacy through MCC sits squarely in the best of American democratic tradition: embracing women and people of color in leadership and within community, while deepening Christianity and evangelical traditions. I consider it an honor to know him and a personal thrill that we share a Leo birthday!"

- Torie Osborn, author and activist, and Executive Director of the Liberty Hill Foundation in Santa Monica, California

For 30 years, I have lent my voice and strength to the work of building a just and equitable society for all of our citizens. Three decades of this work have taught me two lessons:

- We must use every means at our disposal to get our message out and:

- We must not rest until our nation's highest ideals have transcended promise and become reality for all our citizens.

Through the Millennium March, I will stand with one million of my brothers and sisters, and each of us will proclaim:

This is our country, too.

This is our flag.

This is our Constitution!

This is our military!

This is our nation's promise!

This is our contribution to America!

This is our spirituality!

This is our love!

This is our freedom!

This is our life!

This is our dream!

- Reverend Troy Perry, clarifying UFMCC's reasons for proposing, with the Human Rights Campaign, the Millennium March on Washington, quoted in *Speaking for Our Lives: Historic Speeches and Rhetoric for Gay and Lesbian Rights (1892-2000)*

"An end to all social, economic, judicial and legal oppression of Lesbian & Gay People."

The original 5 demands from the —

1st National March on Washington for Lesbian & Gay Rights

October 14, 1979 —

1. Pass a comprehensive lesbian/gay rights bill in Congress.

2. Issue a presidential executive order banning discrimination based on sexual orientation in the Federal Government, the military and federally-contracted private employment.

3. Repeal all anti-lesbian/gay laws.

4. End discrimination in lesbian and gay father custody cases.

5. Protect lesbian and gay youth from any laws which are used to discriminate against, oppress and/or harass them in their homes, schools, jobs and social environments.

Listen to me:

Until those who seek to oppress us have ceased from their ways:

>   WE MUST NOT REST!

Until the government leaves our families alone and protects our children:

>   WE MUST NOT REST!

Until we can marry those we love:

>   WE MUST NOT REST!

Until hatred and prejudice are banished from our vocabularies:

>   WE MUST NOT REST!

Until the doors of all churches and temples and houses of faith open wide in welcome to all people:

>   WE MUST NOT REST!

Until the Matt Shepards and the James Byrds and the Billy Jack Gaithers are no longer taken from us.

>   WE MUST NOT REST!

- Reverend Troy Perry, Millennium March for Equality, April 30, 2000, quoted in *Speaking for Our Lives: Historic Speeches and Rhetoric for Gay and Lesbian Rights (1892-2000)*

For my house shall be called a house of prayer for all peoples.
Thus says the Sovereign God, who gathers the outcasts of Israel,
I will gather others to them besides those already gathered.

- Isaiah 56:7c-8

"Troy Perry is a pastor with exuberant energy amazingly unfettered by the persistent resistance of the church to the radical inclusiveness of the gospel or the daunting challenge of confronting the bigotry and homophobia of our society. To be with Troy is to be in the presence of a profound joy that has little to do with the ebb and flow of happiness or success."
- Reverend John Thomas, Presiding Minister of the United Church of Christ

In 1974, at our General Conference held in San Francisco, when I learned that a resolution recommending application for membership in ecumenical and interreligious organizations (including the National Council of the Churches of Christ in the U.S.A.) was to be presented by one of our new pastors from Boston, Reverend Nancy Wilson, I was not alarmed. Nor was I impressed. Membership in the World or National Council of Churches was not one of my priorities. Reverend Wilson, however, was a very determined woman.

Seven years later, Reverend Elder Wilson was a leader in our denomination. In 1981, at Nancy's urging, our Board of Elders, including myself, agreed to apply for membership in the National Council of Churches. We announced our decision during our General Conference in Houston, and it was carried by the press. The National Council's response, also via media, was swift, putting us on notice that any approach toward them from us would be "impertinent foolishness."

We created our Department of Ecumenical Relations. Reverend Wilson and Adam DeBaugh were named as co-directors. We made certain that we were not making our application to the National Council of Churches for any wrong reasons, such as to legitimize our existence. The Holy Spirit legitimized our existence. Further authorization is not required. Adam DeBaugh wrote our Fellowship's letter of application, dated September 9, 1981. After months of delay, under the previous chair of the Council's Constituent Membership Committee, the new chair, Reverend Dr. Oscar McCloud, called a meeting for March 15, 1982.

"Our first and major goal is to have a forum to tell the story of Metropolitan Community Church to your communions, and to engage in a shared dialogue with all of them," Nancy would repeat on many occasions, forthrightly admitting, "The question of achieving membership has to be our secondary objective."

Oscar McCloud, an African-American Presbyterian minister, was one of the wonderful surprises that we now and then receive in a lifetime. "We have recommended that our Governing Board find Metropolitan Community Churches eligible for membership," Dr. McCloud was pleased to inform us. "The decision was unanimous."

"Meeting you people has been a redemptive experience for our committee," said National Council of Churches associate general secretary Arleon Kelley, who had been quoted earlier in *The Christian Century* to the effect that our reception was "extremely doubtful."

The subsequent meeting of the Governing Board in Nashville, Tennessee, May 12-15, 1982, was described by *Time* magazine as "explosive." The Board consisted of 260 men and women representing 32 communions. Ultimately, it was resolved that the vote on our eligibility would be held a year later, in May 1983, when the Governing Board would hold its scheduled semiannual meeting in San Francisco.

In March 1983, a report consisting of 467 pages, including papers from the UFMCC and 16 other denominations, was presented to the 32-member Faith and Order Commission. Karen Ziegler and Don Eastman were our well-qualified representatives at that meeting. Don later reported, "I felt like the apostle Peter, unlearned because, academically, everybody there was way beyond me. And we were presenting the only thing we had to stand upon, our faith—the faith which has changed our lives." The commission subsequently reflected, "When our churches have failed to extend compassion and nurture, guilt and failure are often expressed as hostility. Under rejection many homosexuals have turned from existing churches and have come together in a new Christian community."

Our Board of Elders agreed that Reverend Don Eastman was the person to represent us before the Governing Board of the National Council of Churches in San Francisco. After his presentation, a leading writer for the National Catholic Reporter stepped toward him and said, "You get an 'A' for that speech!"

The event of primary concern to members of my denomination was the worship service Wednesday evening, at which we would welcome the Governing Board of the National Council of Churches. It was organized by our Bay Area clergy, with Reverend Michael England and Reverend James Sandmire providing leadership, at the Old First Presbyterian Church. Nancy

Wilson asked that I preach the sermon that evening. I found myself looking for avenues of escape. "Why don't you do it?" I said to Nancy, who was prepared for my response. "Absolutely not!" she replied without hesitation. "They want to hear you even if you get loud and scare them. You're the one God gave our message to. You're the person they need to hear."

I worried for days, evaluating what I should say in a sermon to many of the most important Christian leaders in America. It was an opportunity that would have been beyond belief only a few years earlier. My lover broke the tension by laughing at me. "This is when you're at your best—when you don't know the way." he said. "Relax! Preach what God leads you to preach. You be you. Don't change a thing."

When the time of the service arrived, hundreds of members eagerly arrived. I realized I had never suspected so many of our men owned conservative three-piece suits! A female friend I had never seen in anything but slacks arrived wearing a dress. She wobbled from pew to pew in high-heel shoes she had not worn since her mother's funeral fifteen years before. "Don't—you— say—a— word!" the woman cautioned when she caught me smiling in disbelief.
Some of our visitors from other denominations expected the choir would try to impress them with a classical arrangement, something like the Hallelujah

Chorus from Handel's Messiah, but what they sang was a moving, traditional rendition of the beloved children's hymn: "Jesus loves me, this I know, for the Bible tells me so." People throughout the church were crying.

Toward the end of my sermon, I observed:

"There are 22 million homosexuals in America.
In Metropolitan Community Church
we have 35,000. Those figures say to me that
the majority of gay men and lesbian women
in the United States are in your churches.
On Judgment Day, God will ask,
"What did you do to, or do for, the
lesbians and gays who are
members of your churches?
Amen?"

"Amen!" responded the congregation.

After singing, we arrived at a historic event. Most of us were unaware as we approached Holy Communion that the National Council of Churches of Christ did not, and had never been able to, offer the Blessed Sacrament, because they could not agree upon what constitutes the Eucharist. Metropolitan Community Church, on the contrary, needing to be truly ecumenical, never had any difficulty celebrating Holy Communion, which we have

served since our very first service in 1968. On that day, May 11, 1983, two lesbian ministers, Reverend Freda Smith and Reverend Nancy Wilson, consecrated Communion—but being women, their role was as foreign to some representatives of the National Council as was the ecumenical Communion itself. People streamed forward toward the altar. Leaders from America's churches stood in line to receive Holy Communion from Metropolitan Community Church.

I saw a fellow who works for one of the wire services in line to receive, his reporter's notepad protruding from a coat pocket, forgotten, as he waited, crying. I think that writer was not gay, but merely overwhelmed by the service.

When it was over, a woman on the Governing Board said, "I've never felt the Holy Spirit in my church like this. I don't know what you people do. Why do you have it when we don't?"

In the fall of 1983, meeting in Hartford, Connecticut, the National Council of Churches voted to postpone indefinitely any vote on the matter of our eligibility. It was the end of a chapter, but not the end of our story.

One of the bright moments in our continuing dialogue came when an Orthodox theologian said to one of ours, "I think what MCC is saying about religion not centering on sexuality is much like what Copernicus said—that the earth revolves around the sun, and not the sun around the earth."

Galileo defended Copernicus' hypothesis and, in 1633, Galileo, a Catholic, was forced to recant or face excommunication. Not until 1983, after 351 years, did his church admit the error.

~✧~

Early in the AIDS crisis, I was on a program that was nationally televised in Canada, similar to "60 Minutes" in format, that electronically brought me face to face with Jerry Falwell, who has made no secret of his homophobic feelings. The subject was AIDS. Falwell's condescending smile and cloying piety made me cold for a moment, and then hot with anger. I listened in disbelief to Falwell's view that AIDS is God's gift to gay people, just as herpes was God's gift to promiscuous heterosexuals!

My composure returned, my voice controlled. "I do not believe AIDS is God's gift to gay people, Reverend Falwell," I said to him, staring hard into the television camera's eye. "It is not a gift of God any more than sickle cell anemia is God's gift to black people, any more than toxic shock syndrome is God's gift to women, or any more than Legionnaire's disease is God's gift to members of the American Legion for being too patriotic! I do not believe in a theology of the common cold!"

Subsequently, when I was on the Donahue show, I mentioned Falwell's comment, which one of his embarrassed lieutenants vehemently tried to deny. The difference was, of course, that AIDS was always "an equal opportunity disease."

"The first time I met Troy Perry was at MCC in San Francisco when I received holy communion from him at the altar rail. I was struck by his buoyant, loving nature, and his altogether positive response to life.

"In years that followed, our paths crossed innumerable times and on some wonderful occasions. He invited me to be a speaker at the UFMCC General Conference in Phoenix and at an anniversary celebration in Los Angeles. Probably our most memorable time together was as guests of The Advocate, the national gay and lesbian newsmagazine, to participate in a joint interview for their April 2, 1985 issue. Troy and I were photographed together (in ecclesiastical vestments) for what became a classic magazine cover, one of the most discussed and famous in the magazine's history. We were both laughing and celebrating our mission as evangelists; the magazine rightly gave our picture the label "The Joy of Gay Spirituality."

"When my mother, Beatrice, died just 10 days before her 99th birthday, Troy came to the Episcopal Cathedral and sat in the front row at her memorial service. We have spent time together in New York City and Miami, from coast to coast, and from north to south. I honor Troy Perry as a true pioneer in gay liberation, in Christian evangelism, in global healing, and in social justice. All of us are deeply in his debt as he has led the way."

- The Reverend Canon Malcolm Boyd, Episcopal priest and poet-writer in residence at the Los Angeles Cathedral Center of St. Paul

In 1987, I received a letter from the National Conference of Catholic Bishops, inviting me and another representative of the Universal Fellowship of Metropolitan Community Churches to participate in an ecumenical service in Columbia, South Carolina, where Pope John Paul II would officiate. My first reaction was this must be a joke. My second thought was, "I bet some gay person working in the bishops' office said, 'Oh, let's just add Reverend Perry's name to the guest list.'"

I decided to attend, inviting Reverend Nancy Wilson to accompany me. Because we were guests of the Catholics, there was little we felt we could do to address the problems Catholic homosexuals were having other than to give witness to the fact that we existed. With this as our intention, Nancy and I each wore buttons that read: GOD IS GREATER THAN AIDS - Metropolitan Community Churches.

Months later I was having dinner in a restaurant in Los Angeles, when a man approached my table and said, "Reverend Perry, I was in South Carolina and saw you at the service. A friend of mine pointed you out to me. I pastor a Roman Catholic church here in town."

"I am glad to meet you." I said, "Which church?" He told me. It was a church where I had been denied Communion years before. "I just wanted to tell you that I have started a ministry to lesbian and gay persons in our church," he said. "I want everybody to feel welcome to our Mass."

"Hallelujah!" I almost shouted. I then told him what had happened to me in the church he now pastored. When I finished he said, "Hallelujah!"

"It was the year our Chi-Rho cross was beginning to be used. When a banner with that insignia emblazoned upon it was carried down the aisle, the congregation stood and

nearly came to attention. It was like being at a patriotic rally! I looked around and saw that almost everybody had tears in their eyes. I must tell you I had never really experienced the meaning of 'thrilling' until that moment!"

- Reverend Lee Carlton

"You will receive power when the Holy Spirit has come upon you; and you will be my witnesses to the ends of the earth."

- Jesus in Acts 1:8

Reverend Lee Carlton became pastor of the Mother Church when a constantly expanding national membership required me to become our Universal Fellowship's full-time moderator. One of his first appointments as assistant pastor had been as secretary of our board of evangelism (which was supplemented by the board of world missions—which became the board of World Church Extension). When Lee accepted the appointment, it was partly because he was intrigued by thirty-two unanswered letters in my office containing inquiries about our gospel from such diverse countries as France, Italy, Yugoslavia, Nigeria, Denmark, Argentina, New Zealand, Australia, and a few other nations where, miraculously, word was being spread about the existence of Metropolitan Community Church. It was as a result of Reverend Carlton's correspondence that we traveled across the continent and across the seas...

By 1979, Reverend Jean White was elected to the Board of Elders of our Universal Fellowship. As an elder, Jean not only was pastor of our London church, she also became the chair and executive secretary of World Church Extension, an important work that she performed with skill and devotion.

"MCC started in America, but MCC is now a Christian church on an international level. We must never forget that we are Christ's ambassadors to foreign lands—sometimes hostile lands—particularly for gay and lesbian folk."

- Reverend Elder Jean White

"There are few individuals alive today who have contributed to the well being of so many people as has Reverend Troy Perry. His spiritual leadership has led to the formation of a world-wide denomination, and hundreds of thousands of people inside and outside this denomination have been given hope and have renewed their spiritual journey because of his work. Most mainline denominations  *who have wanted to let their homophobic policy remain intact have been turned upside down because of his work. His political leadership has unleashed the LGBT Christian movement as a force to be reckoned with. Through his leadership, MCC churches have changed corporations' policies, city ordinances, human rights codes and led the fight for the right to marry, winning that right in Canada. 'Once we were not a people, now we are the people of God.' Thank you, Reverend Perry. 'Well done, good and faithful servant.'"*

\- Reverend Dr. Brent Hawkes, Senior Pastor,
Metropolitan Community Church of Toronto

"Reverend Troy Perry and his God-given revelation of good news for all of God's people, including homosexuals, has saved not only the lives of thousands of others, it has saved mine. Through the ministry of local MCC churches, I have found meaning, inclusion, and most important of all, I have reclaimed God and the faith that brings justice and wholeness. Thank you Reverend Perry. As you prepare to retire, may Spirit bear witness to you, as She did to Jesus:

"This is my child, my beloved, with whom I am well pleased."

- Reverend Neil Thomas, a native of the United Kingdom, Senior Pastor of the founding church of the UFMCC, the Metropolitan Community Church of Los Angeles.

"Troy is so many things to so many of us. For me, he is our very own Princess Di —maybe a version with Village People New York flair!

The few times I was honoured to meet Princess Di, she was gracious, gentle and yet so focused on the power of good, of making a positive difference, of showing love where there was not much before. What most of us did not see was that she did this beyond the spotlight of the world's newspapers and media.

In many ways, that is how Jesus comes to us, in our every day, beyond the spotlight. The miracles of kindness, the giving beyond all expectations, being there with those who mourn, grieve and need our hope, our Emmanuel—God is in our hope, in our risking for a better world, God's world here and now.

This is why Troy is our very own Princess Di —he too not only is the amazing leader, voice of prophecy, power for justice, pastor, counselor. In the midst of all that, I remember how he, within one day of hearing about my Mum's sudden death, changed everything and flew thousands of miles to hold me and my family. I know many of you who know Troy will have similar stories of his powerful love that stretched out to you.

But love is a risk. I am reminded of Anais Nin who wrote "The time came when the risk it took to remain tight in a bud was more painful than the risk it took to blossom." Troy, I am so thankful for you, risking all those years ago, to go beyond the bud and blossom forth hope for millions, that God calls us all and loves us as we are.

But as we thank God for Troy's ministry—and for his future ministries—that same calling—to risk beyond the bud to blossom forth God's faith, God's hope in us, God's love and justice for all is very much here and now for all of us. We CAN make poverty history, we CAN make HIV/AIDS, TB, malaria and other health challenges history, and ensure all people have access to life-saving drugs, we CAN make every child have the right to life, we CAN make hope not only a reality for everyone, but a spiritual right—a right of God who loves in us.

Troy, you are the blossom of God to me and so many. May your beautiful spirit continue to glow and bloom in joy, love and peace always. From our very hearts, in you, we have thanksgiving!"

- Reverend Elder Hong Tan, MCC's first European District Co-ordinator, Asian-ordained clergy and Asian Elder. Former Senior pastor of MCC North London.

TROY'S LEGACY

CHRIS GLASER

———————⊕———————

Jesus urged us not to hide our light, but to proclaim it to the ends of earth. Beginning with a spiritually abused gay Latino in Los Angeles, the Holy Spirit inspired Troy to proclaim "God loves you" to every gay, lesbian, bisexual, and transgender person in the world. Not all have heard that gospel, thus the work of the Universal Fellowship of Metropolitan Community Churches continues. God gave Troy the message, and gave him the power to create the messenger, UFMCC. The messenger has already done more and greater things than Troy himself could do alone, and yet, there are more and greater things to come.

Vincent van Gogh acknowledged that life is only a kind of sowing time, and, as spiritual author Henri Nouwen interpreted the artist's sentiment, the harvest of our lives frequently comes after our brief life spans. Troy has already been blessed with seeing a preliminary harvest: 250 MCC congregations, and, over almost 40 years, tens of thousands of lives saved from closets, from spiritual abuse, and from imagined separation from God. And this does not include "the light to the nations" that UFMCC has been to all Christian and other religious traditions in his and his denomination's ecumenical and interfaith witness, from helping denominational groups form to UFMCC's reaching out to the National and then World Council of Churches. Nor does it include the social and political enlightenment Troy and UFMCC have brought to our communities and governments.

As UFMCC has recently re-imagined itself, districts have been redrawn to embrace the whole world, and in such a way that every part of the United States is linked to a corner of the globe. This is globalization at its best: not an exploitive attempt for economic dominance as too many business leaders view it, nor a paternalistic reaching out for political influence as too many political

leaders exercise it. No, this is a globalization in which "they" may affect "us" as much as "we" affect "them." In fact, it becomes all about all of us working together in a transnational, transdenominational church. It calls us all to the responsible stewardship first commanded in the story of Eden, not to have power over, but to enjoy mutuality, whether in personal, political, or spiritual relationships. Ultimately it returns the church, it reforms the church, to the family of faith Jesus called us to be: "Those who do the will of God in heaven are my mother, and brother, and sister."

This evangelical global movement also reflects the origins of MCC. When I first attended a Metropolitan Community Church, I saw a mix of people I rarely experienced in the church or in any gay organization: women and men, people of  all colors, religious backgrounds, cultural heritages, economic classes, educational levels, people with disabilities, people who spoke different languages, couples and singles and various examples of family. And of course, there were those who defined themselves at different points along the spectrums of sexual and gender identities. I also found a church willing to be "out," though all of its members were not. Out of the closet, out marching at Pride, out working for rights, and not just our own.

I love the propinquity of the observation of World Communion Sunday on the first Sunday of October, the feast day of Saint Francis on October 4, the birthday of Mahatma Gandhi on October 2, the feast day of the martyred couple Sergius and Bacchus on October 7, National Coming Out Day on

October 11, and the founding of the first congregation of the Universal Fellowship of Metropolitan Community Churches on October 6.

World Communion Sunday reminds us that all are welcome at Christ's table, as does MCC, which practices an open Communion. Saint Francis began his order humbly, with a few, in poverty, a scandal at first to the institutional church, much like MCC. "Great Soul" Gandhi empowered his people for independence and claiming their rights, but also for non-violence and treating the opposition with dignity—all of which characterize MCC's own peace and justice activities. Because a feast day is the first full day in Paradise, Sergius and Bacchus actually died on October 6, the same day hundreds of years later that MCC was born. And, while National Coming Out Day encourages us to tell one more friend, coworker, or family member our identity, MCC has encouraged us to come out spiritually, as well as to come out to God.

All this because Troy Perry's compassion was awakened by a Latino friend who thought God had abandoned us. All this because the Holy Spirit moved Troy to say to him and then to all of us, "God loves you!" All this because Troy stood firmly on the Word of God in speaking to the powers and principalities of this world. All this because Troy had the audacity, the stamina, the compassion, and the vision to see and to help God do a new thing in the church and in the world. Thank you, Jesus. Thank you, God. Thank you, Spirit.

And thank you, Troy. The Lord is Troy Perry's Shepherd, and knows he's gay. Troy Perry has been our shepherd, and so we know we are God's.

"I dream that we can all come out of hiding, that we can all stand tall and walk with our heads held high, because we are gay and we are proud. We will all know that we are God's own creatures, that God loves us."

The Reverend Dr. Troy D. Perry
Founder
Universal Fellowship of Metropolitan Community Churches

Sit in, in the early days

With the founders
of *The Advocate*

An early gathering of MCC Los Angeles members

Pet Blessing

1970 Long March on Sacramento, Ca

Mayor Tom Bradley at MCC
Los Angeles, Ca

Trooper Hall Spree Show in 1971

MCC Los Angeles pastors: Lee Carlton, Jim Sandmire, Jeri Ann Harvey, Donald Pederson and Troy Perry at Jeri Ann's installation in 1978

Troy Perry with Elder Larry Rodriguez and other church members at Jeri Ann
Harvey's installation in 1978

Troy with his Mom and brothers, from left: Eugene, Jimmy, Jerry and
Jackie Perry

President Clinton and Troy Perry. Photo courtesy of *Newsweek*

MCC Los Angeles members
E.T. Thomas and Jack
Halliburton, 2005

Elders Gill Storey, Diane Fisher
and Armando Sanchez, 2005

eri Ann Harvey, Emmett Watkins and Troy Perry

Troy Perry receiving his Doctoral Hood at Episcopal Divinity School in
Massachusetts in 2003

Troy Perry with Bishop Stephen Charleston, school President, and Jennifer, 2003

Judy Dahl, Director of Global Outreach, with friends from around the wo

Darlene Gardner, Region 6 Elder, in 2005

MCC Headquarters Staff: Jim Birkett,
Heather Huff, Paul Fairley, Margaret Mahlman,
Charles Tigard and Jim Mitulski. Second row:
Frank Zirelli, Michelle Horn-Davis, Slade Bellum
and Clayton Vetter, 2005

Rev. Dr. Cindi Love,
Executive Director, 2005

Troy Perry preaching at the Region 1 Conference in New Zealand in 2004

Troy Perry with Diane Olsen, Robin Tyler, Gloria Allred and others, in a
California court over same-sex marriage

Troy Perry with MCC Headquarters staff and friends cheering on marchers at the Los Angeles Pride March, late 1990s

1994 Earthquake destroys Church: Troy Perry with Judy Hosner and Nancy Wilson

Troy with partner Phillip DeBlieck and LAPD Policewoman at Pride event

Jeri Ann Harvey and Gill
Storey, Region 7 Elder, 2005

Nancy Wilson celebrates Easter
with children and their parents
at Church of the Trinity MCC,
Sarasota, FL, 2005

Candy Holmes, of Hallelujah!
Ministries and Delores Berry,
MCC Music Evangelist, in 2005

Elder Arlene Ackerman, center
with her daughter Amanda, left, and
partner Jacqui, right, 2005

upBeat! founders Marsha Stevens and Cindy Pino with upBeat! singers and musicians. Courtesy of BALM Ministries

Troy Perry and Candace Shultis,
MCC San Francisco, Ca, 2005

Pat Bumgardner, MCC NY,
with her partner Mary Jane Gibney
and Troy Perry, 2005

Elder Hong Tan with Lupe
Valdez, Sheriff of Dallas, Tx

Troy Perry with Paul Graetz,
Pastor of First MCC Atlanta, Ga

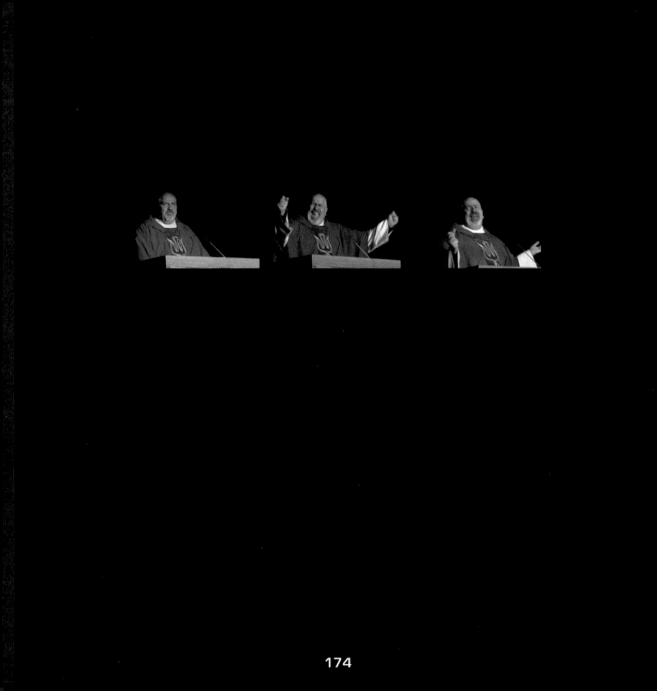

PHOTO ACKNOWLEDGEMENTS

---⊕---

[54] Charles Chiarelli, Troy Perry and John McNeill, [67] Early Board of Elders: John Hose, Jim Sandmire, Troy Perry, Richard Vincent, Freda Smith and John Gill, [71] Judy Kiser, Delores Berry, Troy Perry and Phillip DeBlieck, [75] Los Angeles Church at 22nd and Union destroyed by fire. Photo by Anthony Eaton, [81] Phyllis Lyon, Kay Lahusen, Barbara Gittings and Del Martin, [87] Gary Nixon, Nancy Wilson, Robin Tyler, Troy Perry and Mel White, [104] Troy Perry, Jerry Sloan and Don Eastman in Des Moines, Iowa, [107] At the Carter Center: Steve Fund, Reid Christensen, Jeri Ann Harvey, Steve Pieters, Karen Ziegler, Emmett Watkins, Troy Perry, Freda Smith and T. Edward Helms, [109] Senator Diane Feinstein and Troy Perry, [110] Jim Harris, Massachusetts Representative Elaine Noble, Dr. Norman Pittenger, Troy Perry and Morris Kight at the 1975 General Conference in Dallas, TX, [124] MCC alumni of Pacific School of Religion, flanking graduate and pastor of MCC San Francisco, Penny Nixon and Jim Mitulski, UFMCC staff, [131] The Memorial Wall at MCC Los Angeles, Rechal Longman and Troy Perry, early 1900s, [136] 1981 Ministries conference in Vancouver, BC, [143] Members of Headquarters staff and Board of Administration, [144] Judy Dahl and Nancy Wilson visit Pastor Jorge Sosa, David Pettitt and members of ICM Mexico City.

We thank the following for photos: Troy Perry, Steve Jordan, Mark Hahn, Bill Tom, Dick Rail, Jim Mitulski, Carlos Chavez, Robin Tyler (87, 113, 166), MCC Des Moines, Iowa [104], Jeri Ann Harvey [84, 107, 136, 141, 146], Judy Dahl [20, 116, 144, 145, 162], Paula Schoenwether [123, 129, 163, 169, 170], *The Advocate* [132], MCC Toronto and Deana Dudley [148, 149], Newsweek [157], and Marsha Stevens of BALM Ministries [171].

MCC.
METROPOLITAN
COMMUNITY CHURCHES

Metropolitan Community Churches
8704 Santa Monica Boulevard
West Hollywood, CA 90069

E-mail: info@MCCchurch.org
Internet: www.MCCchurch.org